Diamond Fractal

A Story of a Shattered Mind Made Whole

Karen A. Keegan

Minna J. Kayser

Almaz Publishing

ISBN-13: 978-1490957067

Note from Authors

WARNING: This story may be too graphic for sensitive readers.

If you are a Satanic Ritual Abuse (S.R.A.) victim, please do not read this document without your therapist's direct involvement.

This is a story . . . a case study . . . NOT a how-to manual. Please do not attempt to apply these lessons at home without adequate training and accountability.

All names (except the authors' and Karen's family members) have been changed to protect privacy.

Karen Keegan and Minna Kayser take you on a journey that is gripping, frightening (if you have not been exposed to Dissociative Identity Disorder) and thought-provoking, to say the least, as Minna seeks deliverance from the torment of past abuse.

Those who are involved professionally in counseling, along with those who have experienced the liberating power of the Holy Spirit, will profit most from reading this account of Minna's tortuous journey to healing and restoration.

Having grown up on the mission field, Karen Keegan understands the grip that Satan can have by taking advantage of trauma in a person's life. Though without extensive professional training, Karen relies on the Holy Spirit and refuses to give up in helping Minna discover healing and wholeness.

I recommend this book for those who are serious about helping others find deliverance from their past and experience healing through God's power.

Harold J. Sala, Ph.D.
Founder and President, Guidelines International

Early in my own journey of healing from the dividedness that resulted from childhood sexual abuse, I spent a week with Karen and Minna for extended prayer times. When I felt totally stuck, they always encouraged me with words like, "If you don't give up, God will always show up!" So for hours upon hours, they prayed with me, and during that week I experienced a huge breakthrough. I later returned for additional weeks of prayer with them. Through these times, I not only experienced the amazing healing power of God through prayer, but I caught a way of life: namely, no matter how bad the pain or chaos you encounter, don't ignore or avoid it, but instead walk right into it. This may seem to be an experience of "dying," but if in that place of facing your pain you listen to God, you will find true life and a deeper connection to God Himself. This is what Karen and Minna modeled to me when they prayed for me, and it is what is depicted in their book. Their investment in my life opened the way for me to experience God's healing directly. I am now applying the same lessons as I help teenage girls who are rescued from sex trafficking. I believe Karen and Minna's story will not only give many broken people a new sense of hope for healing, but will inspire anyone to go deeper in the life of faith.

"Jasmine May"

Is there a God? Is Christianity real? Does Jesus heal the broken-hearted and set captives free? If you spend a few days with Karen, Minna and their clients, there will be little doubt in your mind. They are servants of the Most High God who is a rewarder of those who seek Him. Their story is honest, captivating, hard to believe, and real. Possibly more real than you can take in. . . . Creation groans . . . awaiting its redemption. Come and see.

Bill Hayes, Th.M., Ph.D.

Acknowledgements

Although we've dubbed this "Our Story," we wish to take no credit for the beginning, the process, or the outcome. God alone deserves the praise, and we give Him all the credit due His Name.

Thank you, Alex, Bill, Cathy, Cheryl, Dan, Grace, Jared, Katie, Larry, Patti, Sharon, and Shirley for giving of your precious time to read, critique, and offer suggestions for the proofreading, wording, content, and layout of this manuscript. We appreciate you!

And thank you to our godly parents who gave us walking sticks for stability.

Contents

A crystal cut with fine precision
Speaks in silent ways with light.

MJK

PROLOGUE

Karen

My father was a prolific letter writer—by hand, with multiple stamps slapped helter-skelter on the envelopes. Often he used a pre-stamped, lightweight aerogramme transported by jet between Nigeria and the United States of America. Then he'd squeeze his words onto every available space to make the most of his money. If he wasn't writing, he was reading—mostly his Bible, King James Version.

Dad arrived single on the mission field, but soon fell in love with one of the nurses he met there. He claims it was her famous homemade cinnamon rolls that first caught his attention, but I think it was her waist-length braids wound tightly around her head. They reminded him of his mother who had died in childbirth when he was only ten years old, leaving him behind to help care for his three sisters.

His first job after language school was to pioneer a new work in a village where the jet-black residents had never before seen white skin or the written word. During the day he employed workers to help him build a mud-brick home for his new bride, and at night he turned the crank on the 78 rpm wind-up gramophone so the local people could hear the Gospel in their own language. As the listeners began to embrace The Truth and turn from their terror of evil spirits and the spells of the local witch doctor, Dad built a church, a dispensary, a sick hut, and a guest house.

My sister, brother, and I grew up without running water, electricity, or flush toilets. Our playmates were all dark-skinned, and we spoke their native language as well as we did our own. Mom prepared delicious meals of home-grown vegetables and tropical fruits, and we raised our own chickens, while Dad supplied venison for the table. But we preferred the spicy native vegetable stew served over a thick porridge. We lived close to the soil where snakebites and scorpion stings were a daily fear. Our entertainment came from climbing rocks and trees and playing with our pet monkeys and hedgehogs. In the evenings, our family played multiple rounds of Rook by kerosene lamplight.

Here in this remote African village, I began to embrace the mindset that I was superior to my playmates. I lived in a two-bedroom square house with a corrugated tin roof; they lived in a one-room hut topped with thatch. I had enough clothes to wear a different clean dress every day of the week; they felt rich if they had two pieces of cloth to cover their nakedness. When Mom accidentally burnt some cookies, we offered them to my playmates and kept the good ones for ourselves. When we butchered a chicken, the houseboy was delighted to be rewarded with the intestines, feet, and head for his stew. My little five-year-old self felt loftier, prouder, patronizing . . . and full of guilt.

One Sunday morning, while sitting erect on a backless, mud-brick church pew, I listened to my mother telling the African children about sin and hell. Instantly fear gripped me. I knew I had done some bad things, and I didn't want to end up in the fire! That was the day I asked Jesus into my heart. He promised to forgive me for my sins, and now I was allowed to get into His heaven. But I still found it comforting to think that in a few months I could escape from my shame.

Missionaries, in those days, spent four or five years overseas alternating with one year in their passport country. Off we flew to Des Moines, Iowa, where for the first time I experienced snow, apples, grandparents, first grade, and black-and-white television. When our furlough was up, Mom and Dad were assigned to a different village, and I was sent off to boarding school, 136 miles away by a washboard-bumpy dirt road. With my siblings already on campus, I adjusted quickly to the separation, and we kept in touch with our parents through weekly letters. Going home for three weeks at Christmas and three months during the summer was a special treat; but while in the village, I missed my new white friends I'd made at school. By now I'd forgotten much of the native tongue.

Grade six found us back again in the USA—this time in Elkhart, Indiana, where I attended the local public school. I felt displaced and eager for the year to end so I could return home. One thing made the experience more tolerable—my friendship with Joannie —the only other child on our block, who also happened to be in my class. Though we became inseparable, Joannie had some quirks that annoyed me. She seemed insecure and immature yet bold and confident at the same time. We spent hours in each other's homes, rode bikes together, and made snow angels. That was the year my father gave me my first diary where I carefully recorded my daily activities. I didn't know how important this would be thirty-five years later. One more good-bye, and I was back in boarding school, ready for junior high.

In 1970, at age sixteen, I returned for good to the USA—a land not my own—to try to adjust to a strange culture. "Who's Elvis?" I asked when the radio announced his death, and why would anyone voluntarily wear something called *bell bottoms*? I attempted to reconnect with Joannie, but she had long since moved on to other friends. When my parents left for Africa a year later, I stayed with an older couple in our church. Weekly letters continued to crisscross the Atlantic, and I continued to pour my heart out in my journals.

In college I gravitated quickly toward friendships with other MKs (Missionary Kids) on campus. I had never heard the term TCK (Third Culture Kid), but I knew that we who were raised overseas came from the same tribe. We understood each other. We were somehow different from those "materialistic, shallow Americans."

For some MKs, and especially for those who attended a boarding school, there can be a kinship, a bond, between them that is as strong as one's own family ties. The other students became our brothers and sisters. We called all our dorm parents "Aunt" and "Uncle." Through the years I managed to maintain a connection with many of my classmates, first through hand-written letters and then through the Internet. Thirty to forty years after we had said good-bye to various ones, almost our entire class converged for a reunion. We just picked up where we left off. We are family after all.

A husband, three daughters, and two grandchildren later, I still find myself longing to touch African soil, to drink of her beauty, to climb her baobab trees, and to eat Magara's spicy *tuwo da miya* with my fingers. "I am an African," said Kwame, the first President of Ghana, "not because I was born in Africa, but because Africa is born in me." *Am I an African-American*, I wonder?

Karen

Every story has a beginning, and many start with "It was an ordinary day and life was perfect. . . ." But, no kidding, this is what I recorded in my journal just before I was catapulted into enemy territory. Did I have a premonition that I would need this prayer?

> **Journal, June 4, 2001.** Other than annoyance over arthritis stuff, life is so perfect right now. O Lord, may I be as faithful to You in the not-so-perfect moments as I am when things are going well. Protect our family from the temptations of the Evil One and fill us with Your Spirit, ready always to do Your bidding.

Though we never attended boarding school together, I guess it's no surprise that an Adult Missionary Kid named Minna Kayser and I became friends. The surprise is that we connected in spite of her story. I'm glad that I kept a journal.

Karen age 16

Minna

Perfect? Ordinary day? Those words described foreign concepts to me. My life metaphor was a quest—with sword and shield clenched tightly in my grasp. Nothing and nobody was going to stand in my way . . . until I met Karen.

Barnabas Mam in his autobiography *Church Behind the Wire: A Story of Faith in the Killing Fields,* published in Chicago by Moody Publishers in 2012 states, "The danger in telling my story is twofold. Sometimes the mantle of suffering I have woven can seem so heavy. It smothers the message of God's love. At other times my assurances of God's love and favor can make it seem as if the suffering was less horrible than it really was. Neither extreme is true. God's love doesn't negate suffering, and suffering doesn't negate God's love."

Yes, Karen and I have a story to tell, but really it's God's story.

Minna age 18

CHAPTER ONE

Karen

I first met Minna at a weekend retreat in January, 2000, where we'd both been invited by our parents' mission organization to serve on a task force for reaching out to its AMKs (Adult Missionary Kids). The possibility of reconnecting with old friends sounded like an adventure, so I agreed to go. But as the date drew near, doubts began to intrude. *I'm no visionary – "just" a stay-at-home mom,* I thought. *I don't feel qualified to contribute too much.*

I flew in from Tennessee, dropped my bags inside the headquarters' guesthouse door, and eagerly scanned the room for familiar faces. Would I recognize anyone after all these years? I should mention that I'm not much of an observer and have a rather poor memory. I can't recall the color of the couches or who I met first, but I do remember how I felt when someone introduced me to Miss Kayser—a six-foot, two-inch tall, muscular woman with steely black eyes. I noted her face was all broken out—from what, I didn't know—and scars dotted the mottled skin of her arms. As editor of a newsletter for our AMKs, I had contact information for over 2000 names, but I couldn't recall this one. I knew nothing about the country she'd grown up in and very little about the boarding school she'd attended. Our only connection, it seemed, was that our parents had served under the same mission board. I felt strangely uncomfortable around her, yet intrigued as to why she'd been invited to this meeting.

That night, as eleven of us swapped stories around the spacious living room, I happened to mention that I suffered from arthritis. Minna offered to massage my feet, explaining that she had been trained in reflexology. I'd never heard the term before. Again, an odd feeling. *What kind of person volunteers to touch a stranger's feet?* I thought.

At breakfast the next morning, I noticed that Minna held in her hands an English-Greek interlinear Bible. She commented, offhand, that she planned to memorize the entire New Testament—in Greek. *Really?* I thought, skeptically. *Is that possible?* Seemed a little over the top to me.

Later someone made the observation, "I find Minna's eyes very disturbing. Hard to describe—they are like one-way glass. To look in her eyes is like looking at a blank wall. Absolutely impossible to tell what is going on in there. As Minna related many incidents from her life, I got the impression that this is one rough, tough person."

CHAPTER TWO

Minna

Every story has a beginning . . . but I'm not sure where mine begins. Is it before my conception, with the stories of my Great-Grandpa Amaziah Gee (on my mother's side) and his famous temper and years of estrangement from his son? (Apparently Amaziah quit studying for the ministry because he couldn't control himself.) Or the warning to my Grandpa Remington not to marry Amaziah's daughter because of the violent reputation of her family? Perhaps it begins with my German father's stories of growing up in a poor, yet godly, home and committing his life as a young teenager to God's service in Africa.

Or does it begin with my own birth in 1957 on a foreign continent where *home* implied both intense pain and pleasure? I don't know. I just know that I fantasized about living alone in a log cabin in the woods for the rest of my life. And perhaps that's where my story would have ended, had I not met Karen Keegan.

They say you can take a kid out of Africa, but you can't take Africa out of a kid. I identify with the people and the land. I know what it's like to shiver in the cold around an open fire with a *shama* thrown across my shoulders. I know how to eat *injera ba wat* with just two fingers and a thumb, food touching no higher than the first joint. I know how to survive without running water and flush toilets and reliable electricity. I also know that safety lies in hiding under the house where the soil is soft and silky, and that caves should be avoided at all costs. And if I need first aid, I know that the local witch doctor is a master herbalist. By the time I was six, I thought I knew everything about survival—but then I followed my three older brothers to boarding school and found there was no place to hide.

When my parents retired from the mission field, I finally decided to share with my mom about some abuse I'd experienced at school. Her face betrayed her pain; they thought they'd sent me to a safe place. Later she asked, "Do you want me to tell your dad?"

I hesitated. ". . . If you think he needs to know." I'll never forget how he reacted when Mom shared the story with him—I can still see him standing in the doorway between the living room and dining room, his fists tightly curled. He looked like he wanted to beat up the guy, maybe even kill him. His response both upset and affirmed me.

Some time later, Dad handed me a copy of an Adult Missionary Kid newsletter and pointed to an open letter of apology from our Mission Director for the USA.

From My Heart – An Open Letter to AMKs

A new awareness — perhaps that is what happened to me. On May 8 and 9 this year [1998] I convened a special consultation of Adult MKs, Administration, and Board members. During that meeting I had one of those moments when a light bulb went on in my head. I finally understood. Let me try to describe what took place in my heart. First, I have a new recognition of a responsibility that I had overlooked. I discovered that I am responsible for the continuation or changes of past Mission systems. Second, I now realize that I have not been as vocal and visible as I should have been as advocate for AMK concerns. I also know that there are things regarding AMK issues that I cannot delegate to others. From now on I intend to be more aggressive in rebuilding broken relationships between AMKs and the Mission and Parents.

Third, I became aware of my responsibility, like Nehemiah, to confess my sins of omission as well as the sins of past Mission administrations. I understand that in many instances, we have been partially responsible for your pain and suffering when you were on the field.

During that May meeting I felt your pain and wept openly during the recounting of stories, and so I am asking you to please forgive me, past Mission administrations, Mission dorm parents, and your parents when we have not demonstrated grace and love. I want to open the doors of reconciliation and healing.

His words floored me. He made me think that someone actually cared and did believe that bad things could happen to MKs. There and then I chose to forgive my perpetrator, Mr. Ahab, because I knew that that was the only way I could move forward. One day Dad showed me another newsletter and pointed to Mr. Ahab's obituary. Tears puddled in my eyes and a lump stuck tight in my throat, but I quickly got the emotions under control.

I recalled how my Dad used to preach that we must turn from sin, remove our dirty clothes, and submit to God. Dad said when we got to heaven we would receive our reward for our faithfulness. But we must turn from sin. I determined to try, but I wasn't sure how to relate to God. *Why can't God be a woman?* I pondered. One day as I watched the seahorses in my aquarium, I got my answer. It occurred to me that God was like a seahorse: it's the male that nurtures and takes care of the babies.

One morning I woke up in my tiny apartment and stepped out of bed, not anticipating that this day would be a new beginning for me. I remember facing the wall between two bookshelves when I heard an audible voice declare, "I want you!" Beyond a shadow of a doubt, I knew it was God speaking.

But I answered back, "If you want me, You're going to have to come and get me because I don't know how to come back." That statement opened the door for God to pursue me. It was 1999, the semester before I graduated with a degree in psychology from the University of British Columbia.

After graduation, I told my dad that I felt a strong urge to move down to Bellingham, Washington. I could make the transition because of my dual citizenship (my father was Canadian, and my mother was American).

Meanwhile, in September of 1999, the USA Director of our Mission had initiated another Consultation for AMKs who wanted to come to headquarters (at Mission expense) and tell their story. He invited my friend Anne, but she feared going alone and asked her friend Connie to go with her. Connie was surprised by her own strong emotional reaction to the request. So they asked me if I'd accompany them. I retorted, "I will go only if the Mission Director himself asks me personally." *What Director would deign to call a peon like me?* I thought.

Half an hour later, in shock, I received a phone call from the Director himself. "Are you ready to tell your story?" he asked. And I agreed to go. I realized then that, if I'd still been living in Canada, he would not have called me because his jurisdiction was only over the USA.

During the meetings, I saw that the other two wanted me to speak first. I'm an up-front, in-your-face, tell-it-like-it-is sort of person, so I started to relate what I remembered of Mr. Ahab. During a break in the sessions, the Director approached me personally and with a deep sense of compassion asked my forgiveness on behalf of the Mission for the wrongs that were done to me. It left a strong impression on me. Here was a man who obviously cared. His compassion made me think of the compassion of Christ.

A week after I returned home, I got a letter from the Director. He explained that he wanted to form a Task Force in order to investigate the level of need and to better reach out to all Mission AMKs. "Furthermore," he said, "because of your willingness to forgive, and for your positive attitude, I think you'd be a valuable asset to this team." What a shock! I didn't know my life had any value.

When I arrived at Mission headquarters for that first Task Force meeting for Adult Missionary Kids, I looked around at the group. We'd all grown up on the same continent, but I could not imagine anyone here becoming a friend of mine; I felt like I belonged in a different class. But when I met Tom, another hurting AMK in the group, we clicked immediately. I realized then that others besides me were searching for help. And then I spied a lady walking toward me.... My first impressions were that Karen was straight-backed, straight-laced, classy, and most of all "unattainable." I kept my eyes on her all weekend, wondering what made her tick.

In our first session, the Director put me on the spot and asked me what my dream was for MKs. His question surprised me — nobody had ever cared before about my life and my dreams. It made me feel good ... but uncomfortable. I told him I'd like to see something set in place —

checks and balances—that would protect MKs in the boarding schools, monitor caregivers, keep parents informed on their stations, and remove abusers so that they could no longer cause harm. He listened to me and then he shared his heart. He impressed me, and he grew in my esteem. Decent guys really existed? He made me feel like his sister.

CHAPTER THREE

Karen

When the Task Force convened for the third time (June 2001) in a different city, Minna arrived later than anyone else due to a snowstorm. By the time someone from the group could come and pick her up, the airport had closed; so she curled up on a bench outside the terminal and slept with her head on her suitcase. Didn't sound safe to me, but she shrugged it off as normal. That weekend we were assigned to the same overnight accommodations, and I began to ask questions, trying to get to know her. By now she had admitted to the group that she'd experienced some abuse in her past. Up to that point, my only known contact with an abuse victim was Joannie, my best friend during my sixth grade furlough year in the USA. Unbeknownst to me, for years Joannie's father had repeatedly raped and physically abused her. When we reconnected as adults, and she shared her story of healing, my memories of odd incidents and her somewhat strange behaviors began to make sense.

As she struggled with a broken marriage and poor health, Joannie's story opened my eyes to the devastation and long-term effects of childhood abuse. I wondered what residual effects Minna might carry with her. I had no training in counseling or psychology, but I did know that, for me, journaling was very therapeutic for sorting out my thoughts. Trying to be helpful, I asked, "Minna, have you ever written your story down?"

"Oh, no," she replied. "Every time I try, I end up tearing it up and throwing it away. I could not bear for anyone to read my story. What would people think of me?"

And so I offered: "Why don't you write down your childhood memories and email them to me? Then you won't be able to tear them up. And I'll keep them confidential." Skeptically, she agreed she'd try. When I returned home, I received the following brief paragraph.

Dear Karen
 My first memory of abuse is fuzzy. I do not know who (a man, fondling) or where. I was too young. But I can see, feel and smell the place and the person. Occasionally it will pop up briefly in a disjointed dream. The stone walls, silty soft dirt, and the spiders surrounding and watching. I don't know who, but that is how I knew how it was done. That part is branded on my memory. The probing, penetration, lifting and tearing pain, his hand smothering me into silence . . . and then oblivion. Waking alone, a soft breeze and the smell of him and blood on my socks and on my pink-with-white, frilly-collar dress. I put my bloody socks in the outhouse afterwards. Feeling unclean, not understanding, knowing it was all wrong. Feeling horrible guilt. He promised God would bless me because I obeyed.
 Minna

"That's all the details I can remember," she said. I thought she meant that was the only childhood memory she could recall, and I concluded then that something was drastically wrong. How could somebody forget their entire childhood?

Minna

When I sent Karen that first paragraph, I thought to myself, *I'll feed one little tidbit to her, one tiny piece. If she freaks out, that's it — because if she freaks out at a tiny piece, what will she do with the rest of it? Can she handle it?*

I had found work as an assistant editor of a science journal, but my income could not cover my expenses. I lost my apartment with no way to get another, so I found a farmer who let me pitch a tent in his field, and I spent the rest of the winter there with my cat Chewy. I cooked on a small propane camp stove and hauled in store-bought water. Bales of hay around the perimeter of the tent and under my bed helped to block out the breezes; still, I'd wake up shivering and my head throbbing from the cold. I'd show up at work half an hour early just to take a hot shower. After work, I'd return home and let the cat out for some exercise. It was hard living, but at least I was alone where no one could bother me.

On June 30, 2001, when my contract ended with the company, I placed everything into storage and gave the key to my mom. I determined to drive across the USA to visit my sister in South Carolina, then drive to the Atlantic Ocean and swim back to Africa and die in the attempt. I knew if I swam out far enough, I could not make it back. I told God, "If You want to help me, this is Your last chance. You'll have to do something before I get there. The pain is just too much."

Karen

When Minna mentioned her intentions to pass through Tennessee, my mother's training in hospitality and my passion for connecting with Missionary Kids kicked in. It didn't matter how little we knew each other—we belonged in the same tribe. "You're going right past us," I responded. "Why don't you stop in on your way and stay as long as you'd like?" (a Southern USA euphemism for a one- or two-night visit). I didn't know at the time that Minna takes things literally. I wonder if I would have worded it differently had I known what I was in for.

Minna

When Karen invited me to visit her, I thought, *This might be my opportunity to find some answers.* On the other hand, I could see myself turning my back to Karen so I wouldn't hurt her like I'd done to so many others. *Why would she even think it was a good idea for me to "come and stay as long as you like"? I don't know if it's a good idea because if I go to her place, then something is going to go wrong—the least of it would be one more rejection. The worst? One more person hurt or destroyed. But she has some logic there . . . if she knows my secrets and she puts them away where I can't destroy them, then I have to do something about it. So, okay, I'll go and see what happens . . . see if she's true to her word. And I'll keep my word to refuse to let anything destroy my opportunity for change. But what if I really cause some major damage again? I'm tired of being that sort of person: destroying peoples' hearts, taking them away from God, making them fall.*

On Tuesday, July 3, at 8:30 p.m., I arrived in her driveway just as the clutch on my car broke (not a mile down the road, but in her driveway!). I stepped out of the car, kicked the tire, and swore. "You're trying to thwart me. You have betrayed me," I yelled. I felt frustrated and desperate because I knew it would cost more money than I had to fix it. For Plan B, I thought maybe I could continue on by bus—but I didn't want to leave any traces behind me regarding my suicide intentions. At the same time I had an inkling that God had something to do with the broken clutch. With butterflies in my stomach, I turned around to face Karen's house. The two-story brick in a tidy little subdivision impressed me. *She's too rich for me,* I thought.

Karen

I greeted Minna at the door like a long-lost sister, and she immediately told me about the clutch. I didn't know anything about cars, but that seemed a little odd to me. Was she telling me the truth? Repairs would have to wait till after the July 4 holiday. I emailed an MK friend of mine, mentioning Minna's predicament.

The next morning, I pulled out the second piece of psychology I knew: secrets have power over us. I asked Minna if she had any secrets she'd never told anyone. I reminded her that I had no training in counseling or psychology, but I would be willing to listen if she cared to share. That evening we enjoyed the local fireworks together.

The following day we took her car to a local mechanic, and while we waited to hear back from the auto shop, my teenage daughter Katie suggested we start a challenging, 1500-piece puzzle of South African animals. What an amazing inspiration! Minna adored nature, and we both loved anything that smacked of our homeland. As our hands kept busy arranging puzzle pieces, Minna began to share bits and pieces about some of the secret places in her heart. I recorded the following in my journal.

When the puzzle is done, somehow it's symbolic to me that it'll be time for Minna to begin the next phase of her journey.

Minna

Right off the bat, Karen's husband Scott had called her "Miss Goody Two Shoes." *Yikes!* I thought. *She's too good. I'm not. She's going to despise me if I tell her anything. But is it really worth it, if keeping the secret is for the purpose of people not looking down on you or so that you don't get hurt?*

Talking about my secrets was a little nerve-wracking. After all, they'd been secret all my life. I felt put on the spot, again with butterflies in the stomach—as if I were about to jump off a cliff—but I pushed on through my emotions. If this was part of God's answer, I wanted to do my part. So I agreed and a few memories tumbled out. Karen scribbled them down as I reminisced.

> *The town of Sheshamane, on one of our Mission stations. I am almost five years old. It's an Ethiopian church elder. It is one time only. My parents are at the hospital. Mom is having a baby—my little sister. The elder comes to the house where we are playing and takes me to his place. He does not take me from the house forcibly. He tells me he is going to teach me something very special and important. I believe him. Brown skin and soft lips, garlic sweat. His voice assuring me this is to teach me what I must do for men if I am to be a good wife. I smell the smokiness of the hut. Above, I see a spider hanging on its gossamer thread. I smell the* kocho *cooking and the cows. Searing pain, endless pain; I'm too small; he's too big. Then he cleans me and sends me home. (I had hemorrhoids at a very young age.)*

> *It's Sunday. There is a picnic and everyone gets a gift . . . except me. God does not have a gift for me. I have too much sin. I am dirty. God must be angry with me. Then a girl gives me her gift. Maybe God didn't see me. Maybe He doesn't know about me.*

> *Bishoftu, a crater lake. My favorite place in the entire world for a vacation spot—restful for the parents; fun for the kids. From the water's edge a sheer drop and many subsequent similar drops fall away into deeper water. We don't mind swimming in the water, green with algae. We jump off the pier and raft or swim in the floating*

swimming pool. A nearby boathouse contains canoes, rowboats, sailboats, and a motorboat. We enjoy whatever activity we want, including tennis and volleyball. We make the steep climb up the hill to a pool which fills by a windmill-powered pump. A little farther up is a round hut with a fireplace at one end and screen all around the rest of the walls. It is wonderful to sleep there with friends when we are allowed to. More climbing brings me to the rim of the crater where the guesthouses sit. Along the edge of the water for most of the way around the lake the bushes overhang the water, and I can canoe underneath to see the birds' nests. This is where I am ambushed and forced into oral sex. If I fight, I am held under the water. After that I stay away from there when I am canoeing alone.

An earlier memory, same place. Bishoftu. Age four. There are many mangoes, guavas, and passion fruit. I pick one. A beautiful woman (a missionary) sits beside me and shows me how to open it to suck out the insides. She watches me, smiling, as I eat it. We play in the screen hut. I like her. She is kind and gentle. We spend many days walking, swimming, and canoeing together. One day I am in bed with a headache. She tells Mom and Dad she will take care of me so they can go enjoy the day. She rubs my back, head, and neck to ease the pain. I like her. She is soft and gentle. She holds me and strokes me till I fall asleep. She has won my heart and my trust. One day I tell her I don't like men to touch me. She asks me if I like a woman's touch. I say yes. She touches me in ways that surprise me. Gently, taking time, she arouses me. It feels good. I do not know why. I want it. She makes love to me and never loses my trust. I do not feel dirty. I feel wanted and loved. I would not see her again when I start school. She worked down country. I would miss her.

Age six. Mom and Dad leave me at boarding school. At first I feel excited to go because I'll be with my older brothers. But then it doesn't feel so good because I realize my parents are leaving. I can't bear to say goodbye so I go away and play. I do not want to see them go. Mom doesn't like me, so she sent me away.

I have hyena nightmares every night. I see a brilliantly green, grassy hill. Our jeep has slid down to the bottom because it's wet. My dad tells me to get out and push the jeep. So I get out and push. All of a sudden, his wheels grip and he takes off up the hill. And I call, "Daddy, don't leave me." And he calls back, "If I stop now, I'll slide back down," and so he leaves. I'm at the bottom of the hill by a barbed wire fence. On the other side is a pathway. A hyena walks up and he stops, and I'm crying, and he asks, "What's the matter?"

And I say, "My daddy left me." So he says, "Well, you come with me, and I'll have you for supper." And he takes me across the field, and there's an old beaten-up hut with a hole in the wall, and he puts my head through the hole; and inside the hut, there are hyenas that begin eating on my head. Then I wake up.

Mind games, numerous whippings at school. Mr. X. doesn't like my dad, and he takes it out on me . . . and then there's Mr. Ahab.

I watched Karen's reactions to these stories. *So far, so good — she hasn't rejected me yet. I actually think she believes me.* On Friday, I asked her a question: "Have I done anything strange or unusual this week?"

Karen just laughed. "What MK isn't a little strange!" she answered.

"No, I mean like totally out of character or abnormal." (I wanted to feed her just enough information to see if she was trustworthy with the next piece of the puzzle.)

Karen

"Strange? Why do you ask?" I wasn't sure what Minna meant. And then she proceeded to explain to me that a few years ago she'd been diagnosed with D.I.D. (Dissociative Identity Disorder), formerly termed M.P.D. (Multiple Personality Disorder). A friend of hers had reported meeting seventeen of Minna's different personalities, each with his or her own name; but Minna didn't have the list with her and could only name a few. She told me she knew when other personalities had been "out" and in control of the body when she'd lose track of time or when she noticed her possessions had been moved or when she'd find herself in a different location from where she started. She could switch back and forth between personalities and not even be aware of what had happened. She had been told that some personalities liked their coffee black; others liked cream or sugar or both, and others didn't care for coffee at all.

When she told me she heard voices in her head, I asked if she was schizophrenic. "No," she carefully explained. "Schizophrenia is a physical, genetic, and chemical disorder of the mind, whereas D.I.D. is a splitting of the personality that is trauma-based. People who are dissociated hear the voices of their own personalities inside their heads rather than hallucinations of voices outside their minds." I wasn't quite sure I understood what she meant by that. So she handed me her copy of the DSM-IV, the bible of psychiatric disorders.

I took a deep, deep breath. I'd heard about such a thing as multiple personalities, but never in my life had encountered it or understood it. *What in the world had I gotten myself into?* I didn't know what to say . . . but God did. Earlier that morning in my Quiet Time, the Lord had given me a verse in Jeremiah:

> *Everywhere I send you, you shall go,*
> *And all that I command you, you shall speak.*
> *Do not be afraid of them, for I am with you to deliver you.*
> *Behold I have put My words in your mouth (Jeremiah 1:7-8 NASB).*

Minna

My mind whirled. Karen . . . I'm a little D.I.D. I'm weird. What do you think of that? People call me deficient, dysfunctional. What will you call me? Some people don't believe me. They call me a liar. Are you going to believe me if I say, "Yeah, I have secrets"? Well, here's a little secret: there are other people inside me. What will you say to that? So we stick together little pieces of animals . . . you like that jigsaw puzzle, huh? . . . but I doubt you'll like *my* puzzle.*

Why do you ask if I have secrets? I can tell what you're feeling. I can see that you're scared. Karen, one of my personalities likes coffee with cream and sugar. I like mine black. And some can't stand it at all. I think I'll tell Karen the names of some of them so they will come out and test her.

That day we got a phone call from the auto shop saying the repairs would cost $600. I only had $500 to my name, so I assumed they would confiscate the car and then I'd be stuck, unable to complete my plans. Karen immediately responded, "Let's sit down and pray about it."

And I retorted, "Yeah, God may answer you, but He won't answer me, so YOU pray."

When Karen said "Amen," the doorbell rang. There stood a courier with $100 in an envelope addressed to me. That blew my mind. How did anyone know where I was? That now gave me just enough money to get my car back, but not enough gas to finish the trip. Now what was I supposed to do?

CHAPTER FOUR

Karen

The next morning, when I started to serve Minna some coffee, I heard these words come out of my mouth: "Would you like cream and sugar with that?" (Minna always drinks hers black.) I started when she answered, "Why, yes, how did you know?" And "Dani" introduced herself. She began to pace around the room. She declared she wanted to experience adventure, to explore. I suggested she might want to take a walk on the Greenway (a local walking trail). She said no, she wanted to explore my mind and then admitted she wanted to seduce me. Though quite taken aback, somehow I took it in stride. While she talked, I ironed my husband's shirts. Finally she calmed down enough to sit at my kitchen table. She shared that she desperately wanted to get rid of the images that were plaguing her mind. I suggested replacing those images with Scripture. She said she had never read the Bible and could not pray. I thought that seemed a little strange since I knew that Minna had grown up under the training of her missionary parents and assumed she'd been taught the Scriptures at boarding school. My explanation of God's love and the purity of heart that could be hers brought tears to her eyes. And then I prayed with her. At this point, I did not understand how divided and separate Dani's personality was from Minna's. The whole intense experience left me a little fearful.

I don't remember when "Minna" switched back, but later that night, around the puzzle again, Minna said, "I'm dying to ask. Did I act strange today?" I explained to her that Dani had appeared. Minna seemed mortified. *Had she done anything she should not have?* I assured her that she had not done anything wrong, just "said some things."

Minna seemed relieved. Then began a discussion of other personalities, including "Amzie," "Michael," "Tara," and "Carrie"; and the details and stories started pouring out. She explained that some of her personalities were male and some were female. That seemed weird to me, but she shared that the male personalities represented protection. *Okay, I can accept that . . . I think.*

Minna and I covenanted then and there that we would pray for protection for us both and that God would keep our hearts pure before Him. We wanted nothing to stand in the way of her healing and the integrity of our relationship. And God honored our prayer.

Minna

I did not want anything to destroy the possibility of finding the freedom that I wanted God to give me, and I determined that nothing would get in the way. The only thing I could think of was to make a covenant like Abraham had made with God. So when Karen mentioned "covenant" I jumped at the chance, because that created accountability. Karen firmly informed me that if any of my personalities did anything inappropriate to her, she would kick me out of the house. Though it sounded a little harsh, I liked the fact that she had strong boundaries. It made me feel safer.

Karen

On Saturday Dani asked what kind of church we attended. When I said "traditional" she balked. So I suggested we attend a more contemporary one the next day. That seemed to satisfy her. Later she explained that in her experience there were more abusers in a traditional service than in others. That statement caught me up short. "Why?" and "How can you tell that someone is an abuser?"

"The telling thing is the eyes," she said. "There is an inexplicable something in the eyes that I see right away. As for why . . . that's a discussion for another day."

The sermon that Sunday caught us both by surprise when the pastor stated, "Some of you may have experienced sexual abuse as children." Minna said she jumped when she heard that. She wanted to bolt several times, but managed to stay put.

Minna

On Monday, July 9, I began job-hunting, and Karen surprised me when she said she'd gotten an email from one of my personalities named "Lane." I didn't know he existed. I had an amnesiac wall to all my personalities, and even though I could hear their voices, I could not communicate with them; but they seemed to know who I was and what my thoughts were. I remember saying out loud, "If there's anyone there, Karen would like to get to know you."

Karen

I had begun to feel more comfortable around Dani, when a new personality caught me off guard. "Lane" introduced himself to me in an email.

Dear Karen,
*   I am Lane Remington. Minna has said that you might be interested in some of my thoughts on God. I have many thoughts on the subject. But I would like to ask you a question. Why do people feel the need to follow aliens like God? We will eventually evolve as a species to a non-corporeal state just as he has. Do you feel that it is important to emulate aliens? If so, why?*
*   Lane*

I emailed back.

Dear Lane,
    Yes, I am interested in your thoughts. First of all, I want to know how you came to the conclusion that God is an alien. Define alien.
    Why would people feel the need? Someone once said there is a God-shaped vacuum in all of us that only He can fill. He is the one initiating a relationship. He desired fellowship, and so He created man to provide that interaction. That's an intellectual answer. I have the feeling that what you're really wanting to know is why should YOU follow Him? I think it's important to follow after God. He has set the standard; He has made the initiative to reach out to His creation.

Lane, thank you for writing to me. I welcome any dialogue.
Karen

Dear Karen,

By definition he is alien. He is not of this world but of another. He describes his world. Intellectually, I would say he is the one with a vacuum. He has assisted us in our evolution so we can meet him and meet his needs. He is a being that happened on us in his travels and he gave us a leg up so we could ease his loneliness. When we have evolved to the point of species extinction we too will probably respond to some lesser species in the same manner. It is part of the cycle of life.

I know you think I have a bizarre perspective. Take my perspective and convince me it is not so. If you can do that I will be most interested in hearing your voice on Religion. I hope I have not scared you off with my strange thoughts. It has been a long time since I have been able to share with someone who is interested in trying to understand me. I am fully aware of how unusual my thoughts are.

LR

"Bizarre perspective" for sure! I'd never encountered this type of reasoning in any Sunday School class. I attempted to respond with rational, persuasive arguments, but quickly found myself in over my head.

Different personalities started to write to me from various email addresses, and more stories continued to surface. I tried to share Jesus with each of them, asking lots of questions, trying to build relationships, and not having a clue what I was doing. How could I possibly evangelize or disciple every one of them? Minna wondered if she could ever make it to heaven unless every personality agreed to their need for salvation.

I knew for a fact that Minna prayed—out loud. I'd heard her with my own ears. But one day when I asked her to lead in prayer, she flatly refused. "I've never prayed a day in my life!" she exclaimed. I started to argue with her that I'd just prayed with her, but she answered, "Oh, Minna prays all right. But I don't. Don't believe in it." I was beginning to grasp just how split her mind was.

CHAPTER FIVE

Karen

Journal, July 10. This has been the longest week of my life! Each day has been intense, soul-searching, mentally challenging. Staying up late each night has NOT been good for my body!

Minna asked me if she was keeping me from my work, and I had to respond, "You are my work!" God's timetable is not always mine, and He will give me the hours I need. Last night I dreamed someone came and destroyed the puzzle we've been working on, and I felt grieved. Lord, please do not allow anything or anyone to destroy the soul work we've done together this week.

That day I received an ominous email from Dani.

Karen,
be careful of Michael!!
Dani

Thanks for the warning! Who is he? What should I look out for? How will I recognize him? And how should I exercise that caution? What have you heard?
Karen

Michael is someone with a great deal of anger. But what you need to watch for is his manipulation of you, which he will do given the chance.

How do I avoid giving him a chance?

Anger will be an obvious warning sign. But he is sneaky and a con. She is underhanded and vengeful. Watch for grimaces and twitches. That is a warning sign for danger. Do not trust him. Keep him at a distance. Avoid calling him up with statements that anger him. He reacts to anything that reminds him of being attacked.

Why do you care about my being cautious toward Michael? What are you feeling?

I care because you are a decent person and I like you. You make me feel. Your eyes are gentle and loving. You are strong. I am attracted to you.

How do I keep him at a distance? How should I handle it if he does appear? And what would happen if I do keep him at a distance? Would that just be a challenge to him?

Stay calm and strong. Your strength is your protection. Everything is a challenge to him.

I appreciate the insights and warning signals, which I will watch for. Tell me, please, why you switched from "she" to "he" in your reference to Michael.

Michael is both male and female. S/he contains the power of each. The female is defense and the male is protection. Everyone has aspects of both in them. Michael is both.
D

On that same day, Michael introduced himself to me from a different email address.

Karen
    You interest me. I observe and see who you are.
    I want to talk to you and hear your mind.
    I want to taste your thoughts and emotions.
    Are you willing to dare? Minna wants us to be gentle.
    Do you wish to observe, or do you wish to experience?
    Michael

Hi Michael,
    What do you see? Who do you think I am?

Minna is a very wise woman.

You'll have to be more specific than that. Observe what or experience what? I think I would like to observe first.

If you had just one question you could ask of me, what would it be?

Karen

I like your willingness to see me.
You are strong and stand in the face of fear.
You love your religion and really believe it.
You have some weaknesses that show now and then.
I want to know who you are when you are alone with no one to see you.

I'm a quiet version of the same person that I am when I'm with people. I love to be alone because it gives me time to reflect, to journal, to organize, and so on. It helps me to concentrate. But sometimes, when I'm with people, I can tune them out and focus then too. So . . . I guess I would say I'm not much different when alone, just different activities.

Who do you become when you are challenged?

Hmm. A good question. Do you mean "threatened"? (I don't think you're referring to a time when someone challenged me to do something hard—like diving off the high dive.) I'd have to think of a time when I was challenged—meaning a time when I felt afraid? That doesn't happen very often. You're really making me think. Ok, I think what happens is that I envision myself cocooned in God's love, protected by Him. That doesn't mean that I can never be in harm's way, or there would never be martyrs for Christ, but it does mean that I know nothing can touch me except it comes through the loving arms and permission of God first.

I'm still thinking. Perhaps it depends on who or what is challenging me. I guess I have the tendency to stand firm. Is that what you've observed?

What suggestions would you give me to deal with such a situation?

Karen

Meanwhile, "Tara" (who took sugar in her coffee) checked me out that day. According to Lane, she was self-centered, self-assured, egotistical, loved men, was a flirt and a tease, a watcher, a manipulator, liked to smoke Drummond cigarettes, and drank. Of significance, she wore a ring on her left hand. She did not like to eat because Mr. M., her abuser at a local church on furlough, liked chubby girls. Minna informed me that one time she discovered a rather sexy dress in her closet and had no clue where it had come from. I suspect it belonged to Tara.

> *Hi Karen,*
>
> *I am told that you want to get to know me. Well, I am interested in knowing who you are. Don't get me wrong. I am not interested in getting preached at. I only want to find out what makes you tick. Why would someone as innocent as you want to get to know someone as worldly wise as me? We have nothing in common. Do you want to know what the wicked people do and think? I can educate you there. But why sully that innocence? Are you wanting to stop me from living the way I do? Are you trying to capture the lost sheep? Forget it! I like who I am. I like my life. Are you really happy living the good life? Don't you ever think about what it would be like to go all out and experience life as it really is?*
>
> *Tara*

Hi Tara,

Well, I am 47, married to my college sweetheart, have 3 lovely daughters, and a cat. I was born and reared in Africa of missionary parents and came to live in the USA permanently when I was 16. I loved my upbringing with its exposure to different cultures, settings, religions, and people. I struggled with adjusting to America, and though I am quite settled here, Africa will always be home.

Fair enough warning about the preaching. That, I will not do. I'm not a very good preacher anyway.

You say we have nothing in common. Oh, but we do. We both know Minna. And we're both interested in her. I don't know you, but I bet if we got to know each other, we could find some common ground to meet on.

As for wanting to stop you from living how you do . . . Nope. I can't do that. Just want to be your friend and let you know that I accept you just the way you are.

Why do you think I'm innocent? I probably know more than you think I do. There's some awfully graphic stuff in the Bible, and I read the newspapers. But, you're right. Experientially, I'm sure you know far more than I do. I don't need to know all the details to know there is wickedness in the world, and I don't think I would want to experience it. Because every time I observe it, I observe pain associated with it.

I enjoy the freedom from a guilty conscience. I love the exhilaration and joy of reconciliation, not discord and fragmentation. And yes, I'm very happy. And peaceful inside.

Regarding "experiencing life as it really is" . . . perhaps in the past I might have thought that way, but I'm content with where I am now, and I don't think I'm missing anything or any experience—unless it would be to go back to visit Africa. I don't think, for example, I would want to put my hand on a hot burner just so I could say I experienced life as it really is. I'd rather learn from someone else's experience what not to do. And follow the example of those who have found what I'm looking for. Perhaps I'm not a very adventuresome person but I, too, like who I am, and I like where I'm going.

Your thoughts?

Karen

I think you are innocent because I have seen you and read your eyes. They are still innocent. What you have said about peace intrigues me and so does the joy. I envy someone who can be so contented with life that they are willing to forgo the adventures of the concrete jungle.

What makes you so contented with life? You must have a great marriage. I think I prefer to have men without being tied to them. It is more enjoyable and safer too. Men are far too unpredictable. It is fun to be with them. But when they decide you belong to them, they start this domination thing. I won't take that from anyone.

Tara

We had a long discussion on contentment and marriage, and then I asked her a question.

Tell me something, Tara. I wasn't sure who I talked to the night Minna and I sat out on my back porch swing. I know Michael appeared for a while, and I thought maybe Dani. Were you there too? Were you there when I was praying for Minna?

I was there watching you. I didn't know someone would care for us like that. It surprised me. Do you know what Minna did with our ring? I can't go out without it.

What is so significant about the ring that it hampers your activities?

I have to have the ring to protect me. It is my talisman. Nothing can hurt me if I am wearing it. It works. Men are more cautious about how they handle another man's property even if they use it.

I see. No, I don't know what Minna did with it. By the way, Minna showed me the cuts on her arm. Why do you want to hurt her? Does that hurt you?

I get angry and cut myself. I was mad at Minna but I didn't do that to her. I did it to me. It lets out the evil that was put in me by those who hurt me.

Would you be willing to share with me your stories of hurt, and then let me share them with Minna in a gentle way? It takes a lot of guts to do this I know, because secrets hold a very powerful influence on a person. Could you begin with just one? What's one memory you hold that Minna doesn't remember?

All my memories on the street are X-rated.

I'm sure they are! That's ok. I don't need to know all the details. This is for you, not for me. Sometimes there's power in just writing something down. Minna has a hard time writing she says, so I just used the keyboard while she talked, and that seemed to help.

If you really would do that for me I might consider talking about things.

Yes, I really would do that for you.

But I must warn you, I am gun shy when it comes to personal things. I have to learn about you and get to know and trust you first.

I understand, and I agree. It would be foolish to share your heart with someone who would not respect you as a person. Tell me a little about yourself.

I am very affectionate when I feel safe. I like to people watch. I love the German opera. I enjoy horseback riding and boating. I love going out for a classy evening.

. . . Can I suggest that you go back and address the issue of the person who actually did you harm? Why are you allowing him to have power over you?

I don't know how to do that. It wouldn't do any good any way 'cause he is dead.

That doesn't matter. It's not about him anymore; it's about you. How do you go back? When you avoid looking at memories for so many years, you don't know how to walk that path, but the memories are still there. You can access them by writing them down, but don't throw them away. That's why I have agreed to be the keeper of the memories for you, if you wish. But that's only when you're ready to do so.

Another huge step is to choose to forgive your enslavers. I know this sounds like an impossible thing, but it's the key to setting you free from their grip and power over you. [I had not learned yet that forgiveness sometimes is the last step in the healing process, rather than the first.]

I don't know if I can ever forgive him. I hate him.

Ask God. He will help you take the first step, and then the next, and then the next.

And now I have a question for you. Why do you not like to eat?

If I eat, I gain weight and with it, painful attention. I do not want that.

Tara

Minna

I was out of the picture most of this time because I kept switching in and out rapidly. My personalities would only come out if they felt safe with a person, and since Karen was willing to listen and not judge, they all wanted a turn. I have very little memory of what went on, but Karen kept records and shared with me each piece and personality as she learned it. Different personalities used different email addresses, but sometimes they used mine. When Karen replied, but a different personality was out and read the message, he might delete it, leaving the original sender upset that Karen hadn't replied. I felt like I was losing total control of my mind and body.

Karen

After Tara came "Amzie." He was one personality with whom Minna seemed to have some awareness and communication. He stuttered, felt shy, and rarely talked to me at first, and so we corresponded by email.

July 10, 2001
Hello Karen,
I find it interesting that you are willing to take the time to listen to us all. I think it is helping Minna. Thank you for that.
Amzie

Dear Amzie,
You're welcome! Minna is a lovely person, and I'm enjoying getting to know her. I pray that she will find some answers to her questions while she's here, and perhaps you can help me understand her as well. Thank you so much for introducing yourself. Did Minna tell you anything about me?
Karen

Minna said you are very special and caring. She said you are a safe place and I should get to know you.

Are you imaginary? [I was still trying to get a handle on dissociation.]

I am not imaginary. I am very real.
Let me tell you a little about myself. I am Amzie Gee. Minna and I have shared our thoughts for many years. Mom and Dad think I was her imaginary friend. I usually sit back and listen to what is happening around and let Minna do the responding. It is less confusing for people that way. Minna and I talk to each other about things. I wish I could come outside so that she can see me and I can see her with my own eyes.

Sounds wistful. Why can't you?

I cannot because I share the same body with her. I am here inside. I am with her but alone at the same time because others do not see me. I am a calm and quiet person who likes walks on the beach and reading a book by the fireplace. I tend to be introspective. I write poetry and study philosophy just for fun.

What topics do you like to write about?

I like to write about nature in relationship to emotions we feel. I write a lot of metaphors and picture thoughts. I express my deepest thoughts and feelings in my poetry. I enjoy singing and playing the drums. I sing tenor.
I am not sure what else you may want to know. Please ask questions and I will do my best to answer them honestly.

What is Minna like compared to you?

I am left-handed, and Minna is right-handed. Minna is far more intense than I. She is more driven to achieve and to prove herself. I am more peaceful while she is more stressed. I think she got that from Dad.

Why do you think Minna has to prove herself?

She feels like she can never be good enough. She feels inadequate. She feels most self-assured when she is working at something that gives a sense of accomplishment. She was never really affirmed verbally by Dad. He is a giant in her eyes, and she feels like she can never measure up to his expectations. She still has her little girl feet in his giant daddy footprints. She adores him.

If you could change anything about yourself, what would it be?

I would like to have my own body so I can go where I want without worrying about where anyone else wants to go.

That makes sense. Perhaps someday you and Minna will become one and then it will be possible.

I think that I will have to wait for heaven before I can be set free.
Amzie

CHAPTER SIX

Karen

On Thursday something happened that seemed to be a defining moment for Minna and me. We were in the kitchen alone together when a frightening personality appeared. He towered over me, pressing into my personal space, his black eyes locked with mine. I held his gaze without flinching, my heart pounding in my chest. Terrified, I cried out silently to God for protection. Suddenly his eyes softened, and at that moment my husband Scott walked in the door, and "Minna" switched back. Needless to say, my prayer life continued to go very deep, very fast.

Minna

People tell me I can be a very intense person. My goal for my own protection was to intimidate and be as tough as nails on the outside so people wouldn't see the softness inside me or I'd be too vulnerable. This intensity became such a habit over time I wasn't even aware I was doing it any more. When Karen stood up to me that day my personalities thought, "We *cannot hurt her. If she can stand up to us, there's a chance this might work."*

Karen

I seemed to have passed some sort of test that day, and some of the personalities became a little more cooperative as a result. Dani continued to surface frequently. I could tell she was searching for answers, but I didn't know how to instruct her. I didn't understand at the time that it wasn't my job to convince her (or Lane or Michael or Amzie) of their need for God because they weren't the actual parts that were holding the pain. Just giving information was like making stabs in the darkness with a butter knife. But I tried.

July 13, 2001
Hi Dani,

I wanted to respond to a comment you made to me in a conversation we had earlier. I like your honest and direct responses. You said that you were mad at God for sending your parents to Africa and that He lied to you because He said He would take care of you, and He failed you. It sounds like you believe God exists. Yes? But you don't like the kind of God He seems to appear to be? But you won't read the Bible, you said—which is the source for finding out what God is really like—because if you did read it for yourself, you might find the balance to your viewpoint.

How many sides does a crystal have? Perhaps you're only seeing one facet of the crystal. Could there be other facets that you have not faced?

What do you think?
Karen

Yes I believe that God exists. That does not in itself make Him worthy of my devotion. Why should I read about or communicate with someone who just stands back and watches while I am being slowly tortured and killed?
Dani

He was watching, yes, but He wasn't standing back. His heart was bleeding and crying with you that one of His children was being treated so brutally . . . just as He suffered while watching His own Son in such pain and agony. He gave evil men a choice, but He also gives you a choice. You're going to have to come to the point where you choose to forgive God for allowing wicked men to have a choice. It's not that God did anything wrong, but you need to let go of your grudge against Him.

What kind of creature is so unmoved that He can stand there and let a child be destroyed? Why would He place my parents in such a position that they had to abandon me and leave me in a dangerous place? If God is so great, why didn't He step in? He could have but chose not to!!!

I was tortured!! I was raped!! I was dumped on the side of the road for the hyenas to eat. What did I do? I went back because I had nowhere else to go. I crawled back to the bastard!!! God gave me a sadistic S.O.B. to crawl back to!!!

That crystal may have many facets, but it is black and gives me no light.

I'm hurting for you right now. It makes me very sad to hear your incredible pain, and I'm so, so sorry that this horrible thing happened to you. It was wrong, it was evil, and it never should have happened. It's very understandable that you have come to this conclusion. I'm not sure if you're asking these questions because you want an intellectual answer. I have already told you all the answers I know (about God the Father sacrificing His own Son to the hands of wicked men—on your behalf because of His deep love for you. He took on Himself all the pain and sin and wretchedness of a fallen world). I think your pain is so deep that it's hard for you to accept that love. I understand. Perhaps by accepting my friendship and allowing me to demonstrate a loving heart, you'll begin to believe that the source is God's love and that it really does exist. Can you accept my love and care for you?

Karen

The next day I got a message from Michael, the personality that Dani had warned me about. Apparently actions speak louder than words.

July 14, 2001
Hi Karen,

You are still writing! I like your willingness to see me.
What do you see? Who do you think I am?
Michael

Dear Michael,

How would I know you if I saw you? Were you the one who stood up tall and acted aggressively toward me? Or was I speaking to Dani?

Karen

You are very good at figuring out a difficult dimension. I was angry with you for bringing up a painful subject. I saw your fear. And I saw you stand up to me as small as you are. You are one brave lady and you love your religion and really believe it.

38

That's true—sort of. It's not really "religion" I love, but Jesus Christ, the founder of "the religion." So what makes you say that?

Your strength is not your own. I can see that. You are weak by yourself. Without your God, I do not think you would have stood up to me. Your strength is in the fact that you have your own personal advisor to guide you through it. As for my weakness . . . I saw the child in you when I looked in your eyes and it made me feel like taking care of you. It broke my resolve to intimidate. I have a burning rage inside me. I might hurt you if I get angry. Why do you want to be friends with me?

Minna is my friend, and you are a part of Minna. I don't know you apart from her. I know that she has been deeply hurt and wounded, and that makes me very sad. I know I can't fix her, but I CAN be there for her, to listen, to ask questions, to pray for and with her. I don't have enough imagination to understand all she's been through, but I do know that I would be just as angry as you are had I had the same experience. She is a very strong person, and your anger has probably kept her alive all these years. But now that Minna has chosen to forgive her evil abusers, she needs to find a way to release that anger without hurting someone else who is innocent. I see that you are a protector of children. That is good. But as an adult, I need protection from evil too.

Karen

CHAPTER SEVEN

Karen

During these initial weeks of Minna's visit, my family members kept unusually busy, and "coincidentally" they each scheduled out-of-town trips, leaving us alone for hours and hours to talk and share and pray.

On Saturday, July 14, while continuing the South African animal puzzle, Lane began to explain some of the puzzle that was inside Minna's head. Because of all the trauma and chaos in her life, her mind had created an internal structure of order that looked like a multi-faceted, round diamond with a pyramid inside. Each of the pyramid points connected to points of the outer shell. And each point represented a personality. Minna had seen a diamond like that as a child and thought, *That's me!* But she didn't understand or know what it meant. Her perception was that the personalities grouped themselves together in sets of twins, one on each side of the brain. "Lane," "James," "Ronni," and "Ella" fed into "Amzie" on the right side; while "Dani," "Michael," "Carrie," and "Asa" fed into Minna's left side. I couldn't even begin to make sense of it all, so Lane drew diagrams, and I kept lists.

In order for me to get to know some of the different personalities, Lane gave me questions to ask them. He told me that each one carried different aspects of the pain—a sanity guard of the mind. Each had a role. When the need died so would the personality die. He warned me: "Tara and Dani are tough and won't give up easily. Michael is angry, dark, sadistic, and carries all of Minna's pain. He has a vengeful, violent nature and hates men—especially old bald men. He drinks to kill pain. James is a dark personality with a hard heart, but not sadistic. He feels guilty when he hurts someone but chooses to do it anyway. His role model is Mr. Ahab, the dorm parent that hurt him."

That afternoon, Minna acted very agitated. I asked her what was wrong and if she wanted to go for a walk. She said she felt like something was going to burst; she felt very unsettled. When we stepped outside, I discovered "Kelley" was walking with me. She asked, "Where am I?" and "Who are you?" I told her my name and explained we were in Tennessee. She wanted to know how she got here and why she was here. We walked around the entire subdivision before she began to calm down. When we got back to our house, "Minna" returned. I was now beginning to recognize each time she switched personalities by watching her eyes do a little flutter.

The emails kept coming, and I made sure I answered each one.

July 15, 2001
Karen,
   Thank you for your wise input and for not backing down.
   Amzie

Hmm. What do you mean by this? You're welcome in any case!

   I mean, thank you for facing up to Michael. She said you are amazing and she is pleased to see that you have guts. I think you may have won her respect.
   I wish I could talk better. I would share other things with you then.
   Your shy friend,
   Amzie

You're doing just fine! You have such a gentle way and a sparkle in your eyes, it's easy to like you. And I'm amazed at your computer knowledge! I know you're self-conscious about your stutter. You needn't feel embarrassed about that. It's not a defect, you know.
   Your friend,
   Karen

That same day Lane the philosopher wrote me again and I responded.

Lane,

I don't know when you're teasing me and when you aren't. How much bluff was in your earlier emails? Are you still teasing me about believing God is an alien!?

I find it interesting that you gave me some questions to ask YOU:

1) When is it the end? (And I ask: the end for whom?)

2) What do you think will help?

So, what are your answers?

Karen

Dear Karen,

I was teasing you. But I do believe God is an alien. He is not part of His creation and so alien to it. You have a relationship with God so He is less alien to you.

It is the end when there is real heart peace and no one else is needed to help Minna. What I think would help is more of your kind of love and strength. You are a healing influence and your touch smoothes the ruffled hearts. Your questions draw everyone's thoughts in the same direction.

I don't think I want a relationship with the person who allowed so much damage. I am a skeptic with regard to who is good or not good. I believe there is a God and there is a devil. I cannot trust or believe in what I have not seen. I have seen the evidence of supernatural beings active here on earth. I cannot see any proof of goodness in any of them.

Lane

God allowed Satan to have access to Job, and that sounds like a cat-and-mouse game to you, doesn't it? But why did God allow it? Because it was a dare by Satan, and for God it was a sure-bet. He knew how strong Job would be, so He knew that Job was able to handle it. It was Satan who harmed Job, not God. And God put boundaries and limits on how far Satan could go.

It is still a game with humans as the pawns. All games have rules/ boundaries. When you play games with lives, that is unethical at best. So, you say God made us. I suppose that means He has the right to use and abuse us if He chooses. I see a little boy pulling the wings off a fly just to see what happens.

He allowed His own Son to suffer torture. Does that make Him a mean God? No, it makes Him a gracious, loving, merciful God. How do you answer that?

That is a simple strategy that any gamer would use to win. You sacrifice some to win more territories. That does not give the pawn a choice. It is slavery. The slaves are the ones who are sacrificed first. It sounds to me like your God demands human sacrifice.

I may be a skeptic or doubter, but it is not from lack of faith. It is from too much experience. If you are able, show me that He is good. Then I might believe He has D.I.D. [Dissociative Identity Disorder] *and I can accept that. It doesn't mean I have to like it.*

Lane

Dialoguing with Lane felt like a no-win argument. He had an answer for everything, and I fast ran out of ideas as to how to reason with him. I'm glad that his healing didn't depend on my intellectual abilities.

CHAPTER EIGHT

Karen

By Sunday my exhaustion from the stress escalated, so we stayed home from church and talked. That night Dani, Tara, and Michael wanted to go out to the bars and party. I was heart-broken that Minna was in such pain and felt spiritual warfare like I'd never experienced before. I begged them not to go, and when they saw my tears, they promised to be good and to stay home. To help them keep their promise, they shoved a new personality out to the forefront. When I asked him his name, he just shook his head. He reached for some scratch paper, and we began to write notes to each other. He rocked back and forth, smiled a lot, and wrote with his left hand. I had no idea what was happening, and I certainly didn't know what I was doing.

Hi! My name is Randi. I cannot answer you. I cannot speak.

Hi Randi, Keep writing to me then. I'd like to hear what you have to say. How old are you?

7

What do you like to do for fun?

I don't have fun.

Why not?

No one can see me.

Not even God?

He talks to me.

He talks to me too. What does He say to you?

He says it's ok. He loves me.

He says He loves me too. Want to be friends?

Ok.

[Searching for a topic to discuss, I wrote:] I like to play a game called *dara* [an African bean game]. I'll teach you if you like.

I call it manka. We have buttons with it and rocks too. Momma doesn't like me.

Why doesn't she like you?

She told Asa to stop playing with me.

Who is Asa?

She is my twin sister. [Confusing!]

What makes you and Asa scared?

I don't like bad men.

What can we do to make bad men go away?

If I don't talk maybe they can't see me.

Or maybe we can tell a friend or a <u>good</u> man to help us.

If we tell, they [the bad men] *will know.*

But you told me. And I won't let the bad men know. I want to

45

protect you. [I did not understand at this point that Randi was stuck in the memory, and since I wasn't there when the incident happened, it would have been impossible for me to protect him.]

I like you.

I like you too. ☺ Can you draw?

(Draws a profile outline and labels it "Daddy.")

If I could have the bad men locked up forever in jail, would you like that?

He would be so sad.

Why do you feel sorry for him?

He was hurting inside.

What if we could make him good?

He would be happy again.

Shall I talk to him and help him learn to be good?

Yes, and fix the black holes.

Ok. Will you trust me to help? If I can?

What will you do?

I will tell him Jesus loves him and wants to fix the black holes.

OK. Tell him I am sorry.

Ok. I will do that. What are you sorry for?

For not wanting him.

I understand. But he should not have asked you to do anything that made you feel uncomfortable. I think HE should apologize to YOU!

What is "apologize"?

To say "I did something wrong—will you forgive me?"

I forgive him.

That makes me (and God) very happy. And now I want to tell you something. The bad man has gone away forever. [In the present, that was true. In his world, it was not.] He will not come back again.

No. He is here.

How do you know? Where is he?

He is visiting Momma and Daddy.

What is his name?

Mr. K.

Where did he come from?

He is from Germany.

Why is he visiting?

He is helping Daddy build houses.

Is he a missionary?

No.

How long will he be here?

All rainy season.

Ok. I thought you were talking about another bad man who HAS gone away. [I was very confused at this point.]

He comes from Daddy's vilag [sic].

Where's his village?

(He drew an outline of Germany and marked the village on the map.)

When he comes to you, what does he do?

He is older. If I don't do it, I will go to hell. He will hurt Daddy. If dad is gone, mamma will be alone. They are far away.

Do you think I can help? Who can help?

God if he wants to.

Do you think He wants to?

He said to wait.

That someday He would help?

Yes.

Is it hard to wait?

Yes.

I can see you as a grown up. And God is helping you then. I'm glad you know He is with you right now.

Are you an angel? [That made me smile.]

No, but I am a messenger from God. I love you and I will try to help you. Ok?

Ok.

What else would you like to talk about?

I can do the monkey dance. Bukula dances the monkey dance. He is my friend. He is brown [African] and his brother Tesfa dances in the moon. The lioness teaches it.

Tell me about the Lioness.

She is old and scary.

How is she scary? Scary looking?

She has bony fingers. She said I must know pain.

Did she tell you why?

She said my pain will save other people.

How do you think that will happen? When you are a grown up, you will understand.

I don't want pain.

Pain hurts. It doesn't feel good. But pain makes you grow. When a seed is planted in the ground, it hurts. But when it begins to sprout, it brings forth life.

But it has to die.

You are very knowledgeable (smart). Do not be afraid. You will not die. Is there anything else you'd like to tell me?

Why does mom not like me?

Do you know what? I think she likes you very, very much.

She gets mad at me. She hit me for talking. I don't like to talk. She doesn't want me. She sent me away. I don't want education [at boarding school]. *There are bad people there. I want to live with Anbessash. She taught me to write with my toes.*

Do you have a favorite Bible verse?

Rome sast hia sast [Romans 3:23]. *It says the bad man is small.* ["For all have sinned and come short of the glory of God." He took the verse literally.]

Smaller than you?

Yes.

I have an idea. Would you like for me to tuck you into bed for the night? [It was almost 2 a.m., and I was getting tired and wanted to go to bed myself.]

If I sleep, the bad man will come.

So he comes when you're in bed? So if you stay awake, he won't come? What if you slept on the couch where your Daddy could watch over you?

Daddy won't be here.

Why not?

He is working. I have to protect mamma from the bad man.

Did he ever hurt your mama?

He went to her room so I stopped him.

How did you stop him? You were very brave!

I danced for him so he would forget mamma.

And then did he hurt you instead?

Yes.

Did your mama realize what was going on?

No.

I am so very, very sorry you were hurt. That makes me sad. I wish I could make the hurt feelings go away.

If they go away, it won't help other people.

So you are willing to hurt so you can help others?

Yes.

God has a very special plan for you, and I'm watching to see how He is going to use you to help others. Be brave.

My daddy says so too.

I didn't know that I had just met my first "Little One." I had no clue what was going on or how I got in this position—I just knew that I found myself sitting on the floor beside a fully-grown female body who acted like a seven-year-old boy. I did not understand at the time that he was "in the memory" as we talked. The incident had just happened as far as he was concerned, and he felt a genuine fear that he was in danger. No amount of talking or persuasion could change his mind.

At 2 a.m. Minna switched back out—right when the bars would be closing she noted.

Minna

When Karen told me she'd met Randi and how he'd played with her on the floor, many emotions raced through my body: embarrassing, mortifying, uncomfortable, disconcerting. I knew other people were observing this odd behavior. *What is Karen thinking? How does she view me now? If I'm "not there," and I don't know it, I've lost all control of my body and mind*—and control was extremely important to me. I really struggled with this issue. *Who wants to look like an idiot?* But I determined to keep moving. If I didn't, I would be stuck with all this baggage, and it felt shameful. I'd just have to buck up and do it.

In the past, anger was my only recourse for maintaining control. It helped me remember things, to get things done, and to keep from making the same mistakes over and over. It was a key tool I used so consistently, that if I made the same mistake twice, I'd beat myself into submission so I wouldn't ever make that mistake again. Mistakes were humiliating to me because of the reactions I got, and I determined to control myself. I almost never used anger to control other people though—unless that person was in danger.

I remember one time when my mom told me to close my mouth "because you don't want to look like G---" (who perpetually walked around with his mouth open), so I began to clench my teeth and kept them that way so long I damaged them.

Another time my mom reached the end of her rope with me (I relentlessly persisted and insisted on my demands for attention as a child), and in frustration she whipped me, telling me to be quiet. I was five years old. That day I quit talking to my mom about anything I thought was important and didn't resume until I was in my early 40s. I determined to be in control!

Karen

> **Journal, July 16.** I've been through the mill! Way too much to record here. Minna is still here, and every day is super intense. Spiritual warfare. God is working supernaturally in a way I've never experienced before. My body is responding as a result, in tension and pain. Minna's D.I.D. is very disconcerting.

A couple days after the personalities promised not to go out to the bars and they let me meet little Randi, I got this interesting message from Michael. He/She began to open up a little as we conversed.

July 17, 2001
Karen,
I don't understand why you want to lift me up. I have not been nice to you. You are so different from the people I know. I did not want to make that promise to you to be good. Why do you care? I know you have tried to answer that but I don't understand. I saw your tears and it felt like a knife twisted inside me. I don't know how to handle those feelings.
Michael

Dear Michael,
I can't explain it. All I know is that love dwells in me. It's a gift God gave me when I accepted His Son. God is Love, and as His child, He gives that love to me to give away to others. That does not mean I always choose to love. Loving some people is harder than loving others. I'm glad you are able to see that love. God also instructed His followers to love their enemies. Sounds impossible, doesn't it? That's how I know it's genuinely God's love. By the way, I don't consider you an enemy, so I guess I haven't really been tested in that regard. You are part of my friend Minna, and I love all of her parts. It's easy to love your friends.
What hurts you the most? I think if you could cry over that hurt, you could begin to know why I cried.
Your friend,
Karen

I hold a lot of pain. It is all of what I grew up knowing. Aloneness is pain. Intimacy is pain. Leaving is pain. I have had to bully to get where I wanted to be in life. I have had to take what I wanted because that was the only way for me to get anything. I have three kinds of anger: explosive, slow burning, and passive aggressive.

Minna has told me a lot of her story already. Are there some incidents that you're holding for her that she's not aware of?

I have in me the deepest darkness that threatens to envelope me like thick black ooze. It is filled with hatred and anger. I can taste their bodies and smell the odor of sex. I can see the act as clearly as if I was still there in the middle of it. I feel the pain and I feel them. Anger wells up inside me and I want to kill. I take the brunt of their sadistic assault. All events swirl around me and intermix into one horrific event rising to a climax of evil. There is no time. Only an eternal agony. No release. No freedom. Only a sea of evil so vast there is no end. This is a taste of hell.
I don't want to go there. I cannot escape. I cannot tell. Help me!

Can you tell me about just one memory?

Mr. Ahab. He was a cruel man who got pleasure out of other people's pain. One day I was minding my own business. It was playtime. Out of the blue I felt as if my head had exploded. I was in agonizing pain and seeing stars. The pain caused me to throw up. Mr. Ahab had punched me in the side of the head. He laughed and walked away.
That is one story. I have many more.
Michael

Then, Dani chimed in.

July 17, 2001
Hi Karen,
Do you ever feel heavy like you cannot carry the load any longer? I am carrying too heavy a load and I want to put it down, but if I do, I cannot protect Minna. It is still too much for her to handle all at once. I know I seem like a terror. But I have to be strong. I guess you have seen that I am not really strong at all. I can barely hold back from the things I am drawn to.
Dani

Hi Dani,

We all have our weaknesses. Michael said something to me about my strength this week. He said I'd be weak if it weren't for "my religion." But I don't think he understood that my strength comes from a Person, not a system of belief. You can have that same strength, too, if you want it. But you have to want it first. You told me you were ready to let go of the images, and you've already started doing that. I'm very proud of you for taking that step. Yes, it does take some faith, but faith in the right Person—the One Who is much stronger than you—Who can hold you up when you feel weak. If you want to know more, I'll be glad to share it with you.

Thanks for being honest with me. How can I help hold you up until you're ready to let go?

You cannot help me there except for what you did the other night [the night you cried]. *That helped.*

I'm glad I was there for you. What's going to happen when I'm not there? The same God who was there with us that night is with Minna no matter where she goes, and I will continue to pray that she will remain strong.

Karen

CHAPTER NINE

Karen

On July 19, Scott and I were scheduled to drive to Ashville, North Carolina, for some business meetings. I didn't feel comfortable leaving Minna at our house with our three teenage daughters, so we filled Minna's tank with gas and she took off to Columbia, South Carolina, to visit her sister—as per her original plan. (I was still unaware of her earlier suicide intentions.) When we arrived at our destination, I collapsed. I told Scott to attend the meetings without me while I slept and prayed and recovered from burnout. I felt such a relief that this bizarre ordeal was finally over. Life could now return to normal, and I'd never have to face Minna again outside of future Task Force meetings.

I think Scott felt relieved as well. Having a stranger in the house for two weeks was stressful for him, though Minna had tried very hard to give him space whenever he was home from work. I had promised to keep her secrets confidential, and Scott had no inkling whatsoever what I'd been through with her. I'm not sure what the girls thought of Minna at the time. She assured me later that children were safe around her because she has a very strong protective drive toward them (I now know why), and somehow I believed her in spite of my experience with Michael.

On the drive back home, my cell phone rang. Minna wanted to know if she could return to Murfreesboro and stay with us "just until I get a job and a place to stay." She said she really sensed the Lord telling her that she needed to do this.

I took a deep breath. I hesitated. I rebelled inside. And my heart sank when I heard myself say, "Sure. Come on." I didn't know how I could possibly manage.

Minna

When Karen told me they were leaving for North Carolina, I felt pushed out; but I had to go along with it, because what else could I do? I could tell that Karen didn't want me to come back. *What was the use of that visit?* I thought. I figured this was the end. *Okay, I'm on my way east. This is the last time I'll see her or anyone else. After I see my sister, I'll just disappear. Nothing works.*

As I began to drive away from my sister's place, I determined it was time to go on to the Coast, but my visit with Karen kept intruding on my thoughts — a thing which was not normal for me. Normally, once I put my past behind me cognitively, it's behind me. The impression I kept getting was that I should ask her if I could come back to Murfreesboro, and I rebelled against that thought. While driving down the highway, signs kept coming up saying how to get to the Coast, but other signs pointed toward Atlanta. I tried to turn east, but actually ended up heading south. That's when I realized that something remained unfinished, and God had a part in this.

So, relieved that the decision had been made, I called Karen — but I could hear the hesitation in her voice. My gut told me that she didn't want me, but I thought perhaps I could convince her to let me come anyway. If God was in this thing, I was determined to follow through with it, even if I did just want to give up. One of the things I needed was a safe place, and Karen made me feel safe. She reminded me of my mom: someone who listened and who asked questions, but mostly someone who was also one-track-minded. It was an environment I understood. Those thoughts were a buffer that kept me from feeling like I could complete the suicide.

Karen

Minna returned to Murfreesboro, found a night-shift job, and lived with us for two-and-a-half months. It was a roller coaster ride of meeting more and more personalities. Some held rage inside (they warned me never to go into the woods alone with "James.") Some were cautious and watchful. And they were all curious—about me, about their world, about themselves. They were keenly aware of their environment and of their own body. And they kept a close eye on every move I made, cataloguing every word I said, continually testing to see if it was safe to come out. I felt like I was under a microscope of scrutiny—and I was! It was very intimidating. They would sit at my kitchen table, staring intently at me while I cooked, and ply me with questions: "What are you feeling? Why do you . . . ? What do you think of me?" And their eyes . . . unflinching, penetrating, intense. Direct eye contact was extremely important to them.

Meanwhile, I watched THEM. I noted the compulsive need to meticulously fold paper and clothing, to take labels off everything, to keep their back to the wall and face the door. Some personalities had an aversion to spiders and snakes. They all expressed a hyper-vigilance toward sounds, smells, and facial expressions. They seemed incapable of making decisions about meals or activities. And they all had an intense intolerance for lies, deception, and mind games.

The child parts, or "Little Ones," as we dubbed them, were delightful to talk to. I could often distinguish their personalities and guess how old they were by the quality of their voices. They not only acted their age, but they actually sounded like children. If I asked, "How old are you?" and I got the cheeky response, "I'm old enough!" I knew I was speaking to a four-year-old. They were precocious and wise beyond their years, not only because of their innate high intelligence, but out of necessity for survival. They often started a conversation with "Miss Karen, did you know . . .?" and then I'd be fed a bit of trivia about a particular animal's habitat or the meaning of a name. I learned a lot from them. I told Minna that I would never have known how to parent her. I'm sure her mother sprouted a few gray hairs over the incessant questions and comments.

Somehow I figured out that to survive I had to maintain a good sleep schedule no matter what Minna did. She claimed she wouldn't sleep for days, and later told me she would sometimes leave the house during the night. I had to let go of all other goals except the most basic of housekeeping. Minna's presence had turned my world upside down.

Minna

I was oblivious as to how my actions impacted Karen, but when I realized it, I felt bad—like I was in the way; but I refused to let anything interfere with my healing, so I kept quiet. I was driven to learn, to find peace. I felt like a knight on a quest to find the answers to that diamond inside, but it made it difficult for others in my way. I tried to show respect to Karen's family and took my cues from Karen as to how to give them space and not create a problem.

I was never hungry, but Karen would put food in front of me. My personal rule was that if I were served something, I would eat it. It was a form of discipline—a way of proving how tough I could be. I couldn't sleep because if I slept, that's when "they'd" come and get me. I had to be on alert at all times.

Karen

A few weeks after Minna returned to live with us, she asked me if I'd be willing to watch some videotapes with her that might show me how to help her work through her issues. (At the last Task Force meeting, a psychologist with our Mission had handed her a set of tapes for training on inner healing prayer [See Resources] and said, "Minna, you're going to need these.") I balked. I reminded her that I was not a psychologist. In fact, I admitted, I had made a vow in junior high that I would never become a counselor. (What a sense of humor God has! I've since renounced that vow and received my Master's in Pastoral Counseling.) But she persisted and begged me to just watch the first tape. And so, reluctantly, I sat down with her to view the introductory material. "Minna!" I exclaimed at the end. "I think this is your answer. If all I have to do is pray, I can do that. If I don't have to give you any answers—just ask God to do that, I'm willing to give it a shot."

Minna

What a sense of relief that statement brought because I knew these tapes were the key to my finding peace. I had watched them earlier, although I'd missed a lot when my personalities purposefully kept making me sleepy to prevent me from finishing them. The topic scared them because it brought up emotions that they didn't want to feel.

Karen

And so we watched the second videotape together and tried to grasp the concepts being taught. All my life I'd been taught that you can't trust your emotions, and you must live by faith alone. That was all well and good when it came to the topic of salvation. Every night I had sat on my father's knee and recited verses such as *Believe on the Lord Jesus Christ, and thou shalt be saved* (Acts 16:31) and *For by grace are ye saved through faith; and that not of yourselves: [it is] the gift of God: Not of works, lest any man should boast* (Ephesians 2:8-9 KJV). But what about emotions such as anger or fear or grief? What did faith have to do with those?

We learned that the majority of our present emotions are rooted in past memories; that emotion is the bridge to accessing those past memories; that the memory itself is not the problem or issue, but rather that the lies we believe in the memory are what keep the pain alive. Once we'd entered into a memory, felt the pain, and identified the lies, we could pray and ask God to show us the truth. Apparently emotions could indeed be trusted—trusted to reveal what we really believe. It sounded good . . . but how to apply this knowledge? We weren't quite sure.

On August 2, 2001, I heard from Lane again.

> Hi Karen,
> I might not sound like it, but I do want to see what is true. I have read a lot of things and seen a lot. But I just have not come to the place where I can accept anything as truth. I do want to understand what it is that you believe. I just do not see how you can believe it. I have teased you with some wild ideas, and I can argue just about any side of anything. But I just do not see what you do in the Bible. What I see is a pretty bizarre and unrealistic story that people have capitalized on and chosen to believe to help them get through life with some way to cope. But what I see in you is different and it makes me want to understand. You intrigue me and so does the way you think. I may joke around a lot but I do think about things. Please keep trying to explain your faith to me.

I gave Lane some books to read, including *Evidence That Demands a Verdict* by Josh McDowell. He said he appreciated them and that there were a lot of things that caught his attention and that he'd talk about it with me sometime.

CHAPTER TEN

Karen

One day I asked Minna how she could have avoided pregnancy with all the sexual abuse she'd experienced. That's when I began a dialogue with Lassa.

August 13, 2001
Hello Karen,
My name is Lassa. I have been watching as my friends write to you. I can see that you have some interesting things to say about life. Would you talk to me too?
Lassa

Hi Lassa,
But of course! I would love to talk. Tell me a little about yourself. When were you born [meaning when did she come into existence as a personality], and what is your purpose and goal in life? And how would I recognize you if we met in person? What do you like to do in your spare time? As for discussions on life, what topic would you like to talk about?
Karen

I was born in 1970 [while at boarding school]. *I am a person who remembers, and I must remember everything I can so that when the time is right I will know what I need to know. I am mostly quiet, listening to everything I can. I like to hear people talk. I do not have spare time. All my time is taken with memorization of events and places. I would like to know how you live with pain and can still smile* [referring to Karen's arthritis]. *What makes you carry on with life?*

I carry on with life because I know I have a purpose. Tell me about your birth. Who was there? What were the circumstances?

There were two Ethiopian women and it was in a dark hut. There was searing pain.

Did you understand what was going on? Why were you there?

Yes. it was to make a baby go away. my first memories are of the smell of cows and goats mixed with the smell of blood. the herbal drink makes me nauseated and gives me terrible cramps. the wd [witch doctor] *says it isn't working. There is terrible pain as the wd had to cut to help the babies come out. there are two of them. a boy and a girl. the wd examines them and says they are perfect. and what a shame that such a wicked man should be allowed to live. she shows amzie and minna. amzie reaches out and takes them. they are still alive. she takes them back and laying them down she hits one over the head. the other cries and she hits him too. then there is only the sound of the animals moving in the dimness of the hut. amzie convulses and is silent. a couple of hours later they wake and the wd gives them a brown powder to use to cleanse against infection. they go back to school and are late for supper. that means the strap, but inner horror and pain dull the impact. Everett* [a guardian personality] *begins to speak to me. I watch over him because he is blind.*
　　Lassa

Minna

Just before the abortion, I remember Mr. Yonkers beating me. I had protected a little girl at school, and I took her beating for her. My peers saw me as a hero because I didn't cry. Then I got depressed and went to the woods and climbed into the sewer. I watched a snake slither into a hole and wanted to jump off the beam and into the sewer and drown. Just before jumping, I heard soft whistling of the hymn, "I'm in the arms of Jesus." It was the principal. I waited to see if he'd go away. He talked aloud to himself, "What would I do if my little girl were hurting? I think I'd like to hold her and rock her." I climbed out, and he took me in his arms and held me for a long time. Then he asked if I was hungry. He took me to his house and asked his wife to give me cookies and milk. The smell didn't seem to bother him, but I felt nauseated. My tummy hurt. I felt something moving. I knew what it was, but didn't want to admit it. I was terrified. I'd never even had a period yet.

Mr. Ahab had suspected I was pregnant. I denied it. He said that if I ever got pregnant, he'd feed me to the hyenas. That's when I decided to get the abortion. Amzie argued with me. We hashed it out and realized there really was no other choice. I was thirteen years old, with no safe place to turn. I could not tell my parents because I believed they would have had to leave the mission field, and I was not about to take the responsibility for the souls of the Africans who would subsequently not hear the Gospel. I couldn't tell anyone at school because of the deep feelings of shame.

So Saturday morning, I climbed the back fence and waded across the river. I knew where an albino girl lived. I went and told her, and she told her mother. She said they could take care of it. They made up some awful smelling stuff and made me drink it. It started labor pains pretty quickly. The witch doctor who took care of all of this decided to cut me but voiced displeasure at all the scarring. The pain was unbearable. She had to reach in to grab hold of the babies. She showed them to me. Definitely white. I wanted to hold the babies. The witch doctor said that wasn't a good idea, but let me hold them anyway. Then she took them away. A sickening feeling, and then I heard the sound of them dying. I threw up. Something died inside me. I felt like a zombie. I wanted to go right back to the school, but the W.D. said I'd bleed to death. She used thorns as a suture, then put powder on it and gave me some as a wash to use later. I insisted on going back. I didn't want anybody to find out—and they would if I remained away too long. I was late for supper, and one of the dorm staff gave me the strap. I bled for a long time, a couple of months, and it wouldn't heal. Mr. Ahab wouldn't let it heal. I got really depressed and started banging my head against the wall. Mom and Dad came to take me home. I felt awfully guilty that they had to leave their work to come get me.

People always ask me: How could people around you not know what happened to you? First of all, I was not about to tell. It was too dangerous. I had been threatened in the midst of torture that if I told anyone, I would be killed or further tortured, or my family would be harmed or kicked off the mission field. Perpetrators fed lies such as "This is your fault; you deserve this; no one will believe you if you tell." Fear is a powerful motivator for keeping silent. Second, Satan, the master deceiver, wants to keep this sort of thing secret, and he knows how to hide it. And third, some people who hear this type of story don't want to know the truth. Once (as an adult) when I shared about my abuse with one of the staff members, she told me, "I didn't want to see that there was a problem because it's too horrifying to admit that a so-called missionary could be capable of such a thing."

It was easy for Mr. Ahab to get by with it because he would take us off campus by inviting us to go on a motorcycle ride with him. It wasn't hard to keep things secret from the other staff because there weren't enough of them to keep up with all of us. For example, if we timed it right, we could slip over the fence and make it to town and back without being missed. The kids had an unspoken pact with each other not to tell; if we were to survive, we had to keep our mouths shut.

Almost 14, on Mission station, 7 months after abortion

CHAPTER ELEVEN

Karen

By now, my world perception of Mr. Rogers' perfect Neighborhood had been thoroughly destroyed. Lane continued to be a mentor to me for what was happening with those inside, but he also continued to challenge my theology.

August 14, 2001
Hi Lane,
   I've been thinking about what you said about how to persuade you
   . . . In my morning devotions, I've been reading Jeremiah (Chapter 18+). Talk about word pictures! I don't know how much you know about the Scriptures, so I will share with you what I've been reading and learning.
   God told Jeremiah, the prophet, to go down to the potter's house and observe. There he watched the potter making a vessel that got spoiled. So he remade it into another vessel—*as it pleased the potter to make.* Then he gave Jeremiah these words to share with Israel: *Can I not, O house of Israel, deal with you as this potter does? Like the clay in the potter's hand, so are you in My hand, O house of Israel (Jeremiah 18:6 NASB).*
   The master potter has the right to make whatever he wants to with the lump of clay. What arrogance on the clay's part to demand that it be made into a gold vessel when the master knows that a simple clay pot is more useful and needful for the moment. And if the pot gets cracked in the process, how very appropriate and kind that the master potter does not throw it out as useless, but remolds and remakes it so that it becomes fit for use.
   God gave Israel certain rules and laws to follow. Then He laid down the results of obedience or disobedience. I understand this concept as a parent. I tell my kids their boundaries (for their good, for their protection, etc.). Then I tell them the consequences if they

obey or disobey. I am not being unloving. In my years of experience, I realize I know more than they do. I can see the bigger picture. God wanted to bless Israel with very great blessings. He promised them a land of their own, all the food they could eat, protection from their enemies, etc. When Israel refused to obey, and they insisted on going their own way, God had to keep His promise to punish them. BUT, He loved Israel with such a deep love, that He gave them chance after chance after chance to repent and turn back to Him.

God, the Master Potter, with infinite knowledge has created each of us for what is best for us. But if we insist on going our own way, it would be unkind and unjust of Him not to punish. Just ask Tara. She understands the concept of revenge. She does not want to see Mr. Ahab go free. She would like to see great vengeance and wrath heaped upon him so he can feel the pain and agony she felt. But since he's dead, she takes it out on other men. God has promised to punish the wicked, but He is so patient, He has given them many, many chances to repent and turn from their wickedness. But eventually, God will wait no longer. And that's what He did with Israel when they said (verse 12) *We are going to follow our own plans, and each of us will act according to the stubbornness of his evil heart.*

The elders and people of Israel (and even all his so-called friends) got tired of hearing Jeremiah predict doom and gloom on them, so they decided to put him in stocks for a day. Jeremiah did not take it out on them, but he called on God to take revenge on them instead. And God did just that. Jeremiah didn't take things into his own hands, but trusted God to take care of justice.

I need to run, but I want to close with one verse of comfort I read this morning: *Sing to the Lord, praise the Lord! For He has delivered the soul of the needy one from the hand of evildoers (Jeremiah 20:13 NASB).*

I'm praying that verse for each of Minna's personalities, and I pray God will enlighten your own heart as to the truth about God.

Karen

Thank you Karen,

You have given me a lot of things to think about and look into. It sounds like a logical perspective. I will think about these things and then ask you some questions.

Lane

On August 17, I met little "Ronnie." When I prayed with him like I'd been taught in the inner healing prayer tapes, he received truth from God, and in astonishment I watched him "die." He simply closed his eyes and disappeared. (I understand now that it wasn't really a death

One day there was a man who was very sad. He looked like he needed a hug so I went to him and hugged him. He liked the hug.

Later he called me and I went with him to the hut where we grind grain. Then he hurt me and he would not stop. I think that he cannot be happy because he doesn't. If he would stop maybe he could be happy

Randi

Who are you talking to Randi?
I am talking to Miss Karen.
Why are you talking now?
Because she won't tell.
Does it feel good to talk?
Yes. Miss Karen understands me. She likes me.

I think maybe I could not talk to her. I am afraid to say anything. Why would she care or understand? She does not know what we went through.

don't be afraid James. She is a Good person. She will pray for you.

What good does prayer do? How will it change what has happened?

Prayer does not change what has happened. It changes you so it won't hurt anymore. Prayer lets God do good things for you but an integration into the core personality or a melding of the mind.) I never heard from him again.

One day Minna handed me some papers from a notebook she'd found next to her bed. Apparently several of the personalities had been writing to each other, each with his or her own distinct handwriting. Here were more pieces to the puzzle.

One day there was a man who was very sad. He looked like he needed a hug. Later he called me and I went with him to the hut where we grind grain. Then he hurt me and he would not stop. I think that he cannot be happy because he does that. If he would stop maybe he could be happy.
Randi

Who are you talking to Randi?

I am talking to Miss Karen.

Why are you talking now?

Because she won't tell.

Does it feel good to talk?

Yes. Miss Karen understands me. She likes me.

I think maybe I could not talk to her. I am afraid to say anything why would she care or understand? she does not know what we went through

Don't be afraid, James. She is a God person. She will pray for you.

what good does prayer do? How will it change what has happened?

Prayer does not change what has happened. It changes you so it won't hurt anymore. Prayer lets God do good things for you.

there are times when i feel like it is hopeless for there to be any change that will make me normal. i try so hard, but i can't fix myself. i am in prison and i am tortured all the time with the pain. nothing makes sense. life is constant confusion. there are so many voices. i can't hear anything but bedlam. please give me relief. i don't want to live like this anymore. now asa is crying all the time. ronni is gone and asa is isolated. randi is torn apart as well. i need help.
JJ

God is in control and if you ask Him, He will help us all change. He has his hand on us and we will be ok.
Randi

Why would He help us?
James

Because He loves us. He cares about us. He wants us to be strong and happy. Satan is the one who wants us to be miserable. Don't you want to be set free?

Yes I do but you won't let me go.

You already know what you have to do. Trust and obey, for there's no other way to be happy in Jesus. You can do that too, Jodi. We all have to choose.
Randi

If those notes sound confusing, you can imagine what it felt like to have various personalities switching in and out rapidly in my presence. At least when something was in writing, I had more time to digest it. Later that day, Lane responded to my dialogue about Jeremiah at the potter's house.

Dear Karen

It seems that you are saying that all we have to do is submit and let God do the work. What does that mean in terms of everyday life, relationships, and memories?

LR

Very good question, Lane. Someone once quipped, "Pray as if everything depended on God; work as if everything depended on you." I'm not sure anyone has found just the right balance between doing and waiting. With regard to healing of memories, I think God does the actual healing. Just as He designed our bodies to naturally heal themselves when wounded superficially (like a cut or bruise or a scrape), most emotional hurts eventually work themselves out (the little bumps and bruises of rubbing shoulders with humanity). If someone cuts me off in traffic, for example, I might not like it, but I can let it go and not have it consume me for the rest of my life.

But big trauma, like a gaping wound or gash from a car accident may require a physician's assistance to clean out the dirt and close the wound so the body can begin to heal. A friend, counselor, pastor, or trained psychologist each has his or her place in helping a person to clean out the mud and close the wound; but ultimately, it's God's job to do the healing. And, yes, healing takes time. And, yes, some scars may remain if the wound is large, but the physical pain usually disappears over time.

Relationships? If I do something to offend someone, and I know I'm guilty of doing so, it is my responsibility to ask forgiveness. But I also ask God's forgiveness for that offense, because it breaks His law of righteousness. I do the work of asking forgiveness. He does the work of granting it.

If someone else does something wrong toward me, I have a choice of overlooking it (if I can)—and usually will if I can chalk it up to their blindness or ignorance or whatever. (e.g. Someone from another culture might break a taboo from my society, but I understand why they did it and excuse him.) But, if the offense is large (e.g. abuse, theft) I might struggle a little harder to forgive. That's when I call on God to help me overcome the desire for revenge, to forgive the person his debt to me, because I know God has forgiven my debt to Him.

Did that begin to answer your question?

Yes that helps. Now I have to rebuild my life because someone disassembled it. It has been like this too long. I think that logic cannot explain God or His ways. That will always be a frustration for me.

Lane

August 24, 2001
Hi Lane,

I've been thinking about your statement. I agree that logic can only take one so far in understanding God. First of all, our minds are too finite, and His too infinite to be able to understand everything. Frankly, I would not want to worship a God whom I created myself, because then I would be more intelligent than He is! I prefer a God who knows the end from the beginning and who knows what's best for me. I trust Him to guide and direct me through life.

On the other hand, our faith is not a leap in the dark. It is a reasonable faith, based on the historical, provable fact that Jesus walked this earth and rose from the dead. Either He was who He said He was—the Son of God—or He was a lunatic. It's more logical to walk through the evidence and believe than to try to excuse all the miracles away. Again, *Evidence That Demands a Verdict* was a powerful tool for aiding my belief.

Karen

August 26, 2001
Hi Karen,

I think I understand a little bit. I finished the books you gave me. There is little proof that can convince a scientist but lots of proof to convince a man. The scientist blinds himself with his own knowledge, and a man wants to fill the hole designed for faith. For me, understanding can only come from experience and experience can make faith grow or fade. You speak about a relationship that God desires with man. That strikes a chord with me. I want a relationship with someone bigger than I am . . . someone who wants to know me. That is Minna's biggest hunger.

Lane

Lane wasn't the only one who listened and processed information. On August 24, I wrote to Tara:

"Asa" told me that you listened to some of the inner healing videotapes. What did you think? Did you learn anything?

The message I got was that it wasn't my fault and that God loves me. He said it was ok and that the feelings are legitimate. He said God forgives me and I don't have to live like this anymore. I almost am persuaded.
Tara

But other personalities were more resistant. The next day, Asa told me that James had been watching a segment of a movie that portrayed someone being tortured. It excited him. Asa wanted to know why James was that way. "Why shouldn't I watch that movie?" James retorted. Later that evening, James appeared again, menacing and angry: "I refuse to die."

I recorded on August 26, 2001, 3:30 a.m., that James "died" screaming (at the same time as Michael). [James was a con artist, however. He pretended several times over the years that his job was done, but he continued to resurface.]

Two weeks later Asa and Randi integrated following a viewing of Tape #3. By the way, we do NOT recommend practicing inner healing prayer without being fully trained, but God overlooked our ignorance and used a willing heart. It's all about Him after all. Each time we got stuck, we'd watch the next tape in the series, get an answer, and keep on working.

CHAPTER TWELVE

Karen

> **Journal.** I'm on a search for truth about demons and their
> power over us—on behalf of a friend who is struggling with
> inordinate fears. I'm reading Wilbur O'Donovan's *Biblical Christi-*
> *anity in African Perspective,* 2nd Ed., printed by Paternoster Press
> in Carlisle, UK, 1995. First, regarding angels, O'Donovan says,
> "Angels deliver Christians from human and demonic danger
> . . . [then] why [do they] rescue God's people in some situations
> but not in others? . . . Hebrews tells us that some heroes of the
> faith had dramatic escapes from death but others were allowed
> to glorify God through suffering and death. . . . The important
> thing is not whether we live or die, but that whether we live or
> die, Jesus Christ might be exalted through what takes place." He
> goes on to say, "Angels are often the agents through whom God
> answers prayer . . . prayer plays a very important part in whether
> or not God's angels are free to work . . . one way we may resist the
> devil's attack is through prayer. If we fail to pray, we may leave
> ourselves unprotected by God's angels."

I'll never forget the first time I learned about demonic involvement in
the life of an abuse victim. The videotapes had taught us some practical
tips and guidelines on how to handle the situation when and if it arose.
I felt unprepared, petrified really, in anticipation of such an encounter.
I took copious notes, practiced what to do and say, and prayed like
crazy. After my first experiential encounter with the demonic, however,

I felt at peace. I now knew my authority came from Jesus Christ and that I didn't have to be afraid or intimidated.

Minna

People often ask if a believer can be possessed or oppressed by demons. Whole books have been written on this subject (see Resources), but in a nutshell our understanding is we are tri-part beings. The spirit is regenerated at the point of salvation, and light and darkness cannot exist in the same place. But at the point of salvation, the mind still needs renewal (Romans 12:1, 2). We are still infested with a bunch of lies that need God's truth. It's in the mind where the battle rages, and this is where we can choose to believe God or accept Satan's lies. In truth, God defeated Satan at the cross and stripped him of his power in the life of the believer. Generally, we don't need to go after the demon but rather to go after the lie that the demon is holding onto there in the mind. Once the lie is replaced with truth, the demon has nothing to hold onto, and it's easy to tell it to leave.

The will of a child who is molested has been preempted by the will of the perpetrator. But invariably, she will begin to listen to and believe lies such as "I'm dirty; I'm worthless; it was my fault." (The truth is she is clean, precious, and guilt-free in God's eyes.) It is at this point that the demonic grabs hold and attaches itself in her mind and a stronghold is born. Eventually she will self-destruct — until she allows the Holy Spirit to replace her lies with His truth.

Occasionally, if a demon tries to interfere, we'll command it (in Jesus' Name of course) to remain quiet, and then work through why the person is trying to avoid going to a memory or the place of pain. We never give second chances to obey, as demons are masters at mind games.

Some have ignorantly (and harmfully) accused D.I.D. personalities of being demons. Not true. They are simply parts of the original mind that have compartmentalized themselves to handle the pain. To complicate things, some personalities can actually pretend to be demons to keep us from going to the memory . . . but a simple Biblical test will reveal the truth.

> *Do not believe every spirit, but test the spirits to see whether they are from God, because many false prophets have gone out into the world.* **This is how you can recognize the Spirit of God: Every spirit that acknowledges that Jesus Christ has come in the flesh is from God, but every spirit that does not acknowledge Jesus is not from God.** *This is the spirit of the antichrist, which you have heard is coming and even now is already in the world. You, dear children, are from God and have overcome them, because the one who is in you is greater than the one who is in the world (1John 4:1-4 NIV).*

We ask the personality to repeat the words, "Jesus Christ is come in the flesh." If he/she is capable of doing so, it's a sure bet, he/she is not a demon.

Karen

Something else that I began to grasp was the difference between sinful, choice emotions (such as revengeful feelings, unforgiveness, hatred, bitterness, jealousy, or resentment) and involuntary emotions (such as fear, hurt, disgust, shock, or loneliness) that are often held in place — long after the initial event — by the lies we believe. Holding on to choice emotions can keep a person from hearing from the Lord and moving forward in the healing journey. Sometimes people will deliberately choose to give up the sinful emotion, but often they have to work through the pain first, before they are able or willing to let go of the sin.

Understanding anger was a little trickier for me. I knew that Jesus got angry at the money changers in the temple, and I knew the Scripture about not letting the sun go down on your wrath. It also said, *In your anger do not sin (Ephesians 4:26 NIV).* So when does anger become sinful? Righteous anger is appropriate when there's injustice or abuse, but we humans have a hard time keeping that anger from turning into sinful emotions. Oftentimes Jesus asks a victim if she's willing to let Him hold the anger so she doesn't have to.

Some anger is by choice—used as a protection or cover-up for a deeper or more painful emotion. Feeling anger is a lot safer than feeling vulnerable. Sometimes, if she's willing, a person can set aside the anger, and we're able to move forward. Other times, we have to work through the pain first before the anger will dissipate.

I also had to grasp the difference between an emotion (such as feelings of worthlessness or dirtiness) and a belief (I am worthless; I am dirty). We learned that we had to follow the emotion in the memory to find the belief, and then God could speak truth into the heart. Satan is the accuser, the deceiver, the Father of Lies. (You'll never amount to anything; you can't do anything right; you deserved it.) Jesus will always tell the truth. (You are precious; you are clean; it's not your fault; I am with you always.)

I made lots of mistakes in the beginning as I tried to apply all that I'd learned. But the Alters were gracious and forgiving because they knew that my heart and my motives were pure.

Journal, August 30, 2001. Two more of M's personalities "died" yesterday. It's been quite an experience to say the least! It's hard to concentrate on anything else at times. Danger—pride—thinking I've done something when it's God all the way. "I, being in the way, God led me." I didn't ask for this assignment. I was given it, dumped in my lap.

CHAPTER THIRTEEN

Karen

Amzie was still an enigma to me. One day he complained of feeling invisible, and I asked what that was like for him.

> *No one recognizes that you exist and so they can ignore your needs. If I do something that is not what Minna would do, they think she is weird or something. I have to keep quiet so she does not get hurt by others' comments. The only people I can talk to as me, are you and Minna. That is a pretty small circle. If I want something to be said without confusion, I need to ask Minna to say it. My stutter is so pronounced that most people do not understand why, when Minna is so eloquent. It is not positive to feel alone.*
>
> *I have managed OK in the past, but sometimes it hurts. It really hurt when Mom said I didn't exist. It was painful for me and for Minna. Mom just didn't understand. It is the outside package that people see, so that is the basis for all their judgments when they see something different about us.*
>
> *Ah, well. I guess that is how it always was, so it will always be. There is no use complaining about it.*
>
> *I could go on and on about the things that bother me. But that would not effect any change.*
>
> *You are a gentle heart and a good friend.*
> *Amzie*

> *September 1, 2001*
> *Dear Karen,*
> *I only got a couple of hours' sleep last night. There is too much to think about. When I woke up this morning I saw that my hands were swollen the way they used to get when I was tied up by Mr. Ahab, and my throat had red finger marks on them.*
> *I don't like this memory stuff. It feels better not thinking or remembering. I am feeling very depressed and would like to end it all.*
> *Amzie*

September 2, 2001
Karen,

I can't take it anymore. It just plays over and over in my mind. It makes me feel like I want to lash out at all of the people that hurt us. I am angry and filled with hate. I want to do to them what they did to us. I feel sick. I have to let the sickness out somehow. I don't want to feel like this. I can't help it. It just pours over me like a tidal wave taking me with it. Help me. Help me to stop the raging fire. It burns. I am evil. I don't want to be. Here's a poem I wrote this morning.

Voices of Duplicity
By Amzie Gee

Voices of many speaking duplicity
Alone, lonely, tormented hearts and minds
Desperately seeking, fearfully hiding
Holding pain in lover's hands
Crying out in twisted dichotomy
Attending, detaining, protecting, profaning
Angered defending, gingerly reaching
Gnarled fingers clutching torn heartstrings

Two hearts alone in a cavernous exile
Many minds speaking
Devoured by pain, hate, lust and denial
No freedom
Sentenced to torment

One voice has spoken to two in the darkness.
Lover's hands open offering pain's heartbeat
The voices are quieted; peace blankets all
Flame's light revealed truth; lies flee at its presence.
No longer consumed by torments in darkness.
Joy unspeakable! Freedom at last!

That day I discovered that Amzie had cut himself. I thought, *What a bizarre and painful thing to do!* "Why would you do that to yourself?" I asked.

"To release the pain," he replied. *Huh?* Didn't make any sense to me. *Wouldn't that cause more pain?* I had so much more to learn about this business of emotional healing.

On September 5, Lane and Dani "disappeared." The lewd pictures had disappeared as well, and Minna reported the first peace, calm, and quiet she could ever remember. Each personality "died" quietly, many saying good-bye to me before they left. A simple closing of the eyes, and they were gone. Each one had to find the myth or lie that birthed them, and once their purpose for being no longer existed, they were ready to go. Dani and Lane didn't leave until they were sure that Amzie and Minna were okay and would not harm themselves and had sufficiently processed their memories to be able to handle them emotionally.

> **Journal.** Minna is continuing to make huge strides. As of last night, we were down to four personalities (out of a dozen or so, plus sixteen fragments). What an incredible thing to watch! Every prayer I pray in her presence seems to go straight to heaven. God's presence feels so real. This whole experience is surreal. Every step has been God-driven—from the day her clutch went out on her car to today with her wholeness starting to happen. What a trip! And it's all happening right here in this house under our noses . . . and I've learned about myself in the process. It's God's work. I'm simply an instrument, a conduit. I've simply been in the way and been obedient to what God asked me to do.

Minna

What a relief to know that I was now gaining some semblance of order and control in my life. I became less and less hampered by alternate personalities stealing my time and using my body to live out their lives without my knowledge. I began to think there might be some light at the end of the tunnel.

Karen

> **Journal, September 7.** Celebrate! Yesterday the last of Minna's personalities disappeared! Whole! Healed! It's truly the most amazing thing I've ever witnessed. If I tried to tell Minna's story,

there would be few who would believe me or understand. I've lived it for two months now, processing little by little. How can I expect others to grasp it immediately? When I broached the subject with two other people, I got little or no support or understanding. I feel a little like Jeremiah in his frustration with people who disbelieved his message. But then I talk to people who have lived with or been exposed to D.I.D., and they immediately identify and understand. That brings affirmation. Meanwhile, I must learn to keep my mouth shut to those who have no ears to hear.

We smile now as we read that triumphal declaration. Little did we know that there would be another chapter of beginning. The outer shell of the secret diamond had only begun to crack. The very next day, another grouping of personalities surfaced. "Jordan" came out to tell about an experience at age 3 ½, and pretty soon "Kendra," "Timmy," and "Amy" arrived.

September 14, 2001. Misty was a deaf Little One, so we communicated on paper. I still kept trying to grasp the concept of inner healing prayer.

Who are you?

A friend of Minna's.

What is happening?

Minna wants you to remember what happened to you. How old are you?

10

What happened?

He tied me up.

And where were you?

At Grandma's grave. (She scratches at her face)

Why does your face feel itchy?

Grass

Were you all alone?

Yes.

Tell me what you're feeling right now.

Itchy and my wrists hurt and my neck and chest. I'm scared he is going to kill me. I heard his gun.

What else?

I feel dirty. Whenever I hurt I am alone. I want to die. . . . Do I have to tell?

You can tell me. I am a safe person.

I didn't ask him to do it!

I know.

You believe me?

YES! It was not your fault. [Later I learned to let Jesus tell the truth to the child.]

I feel like it is.

What would help you feel safe?

To go far away.

What would make you feel clean again?

I wash and scrub all the time.

I mean clean on the inside—in your heart?

If I bleed it helps. [self-cutting]

"Lord Jesus, help her to understand the myth that is holding her captive. Help her to feel Your truth and experience it personally. And give me wisdom to know what to say or do to help her understand." Misty, how can I help you?

You just did. [Apparently she listened to my prayer and then listened for God's answer.]

Over the next few weeks, more and more personalities popped out till we'd counted 130 who had heard truth from God and integrated. We wondered how many more surprises we'd find inside the diamond.

Minna

Some of the abuse and trauma happened at boarding school, some on furlough, and some on the Mission station at the hands of the nationals and from visitors from other countries. I felt like I had a sign on my back saying, "Come and get me." My boundaries had been crushed and trampled, and I was unable to fight back and say no. I became an easy target for further abuse.

At boarding school, Mr. Ahab was sadistic and cruel and molested me in between classes every day. During a math exam one day, all of a sudden he grabbed both my hands, disjointed the knuckles, and made me stand with my nose up against a pillar . . . and then failed me for the exam. No explanation. I was not allowed to complain or tell anyone the truth about it. The hands were never tended to.

He used knives, a broom handle, and a glass bottle (that broke) in my vagina until I bled. Seeing blood seemed to excite him. He pinched my shoulder muscles, pulled hard on my ear, used whips, and always smelled of lavender. I also remember the smell of wet burlap from the school garage. He made me fully undress there. (He preferred dresses — which is why I never liked to wear them. They represented immodesty to me.) I could feel his excitement in the possibility of getting caught there.

One time he took a two-by-four and smacked me over the head. He knew how to pull up a nail and put salt under it and put it back down so it would hurt for a long time. He must have been in some war as he knew torture techniques.

He took me under the stairs behind the classroom and kicked me while I was on the floor. I didn't dare make a sound. Then he tied my hands behind my back with thick ropes, splayed my legs, and tied them to two posts and raped me.

One time he required that I watch him and his wife having sex. (Mrs. Ahab was as much a victim as I was.) He wouldn't let me look away. Then he made me masturbate in front of him.

On Saturdays, he would take me to play tennis, then give me a motorcycle ride into town to a place behind the *markato* (market) to a long, low hut (a harlot's house), where he sold me to Ethiopian men to group rape me. One time he told me to take my clothes off, but I didn't want to, so he hit me. I took them off. There were six men. They wanted to watch me with Alganish (a slave woman). They told us what to do. It was extremely embarrassing, and I felt shame and guilt. Then the men started to take us. My personalities Tara and Jodi took the abuse for me. One guy liked to bite. They used every orifice I had. When the men had had their fun, they went into the other room to have something to eat and drink. Alganish cried. I held her. Three more men came in, and it started all over again. One man pulled Alganish to one side and cut open her stomach. Then they left her on the floor to die. Mr. Ahab got mad and took me out of there. Mr. Ahab blamed me for Alganish's death. He had to pay for her. It hurt to move. I had to fight to keep from throwing up. Mr. Ahab beat me up, and on the way back to school he dumped me off on the side of the road. I crawled off the road and into a ditch where I hid for the night, listening to the hyenas. The next morning I crawled back to school where I got a whipping for having run away.

CHAPTER FOURTEEN

Karen

Minna moved into her own apartment in mid-September, and I thought life might now return to some semblance of order. But 9-11 had just occurred, and my African birth-town experienced riots. Wars and rumors of wars on the outside were raging while the battle for Minna's mind continued. A VeggieTale song from the children's movie *Where's God When I'm S-Scared?* kept running through my head:

> *God is bigger than the Bogeyman;*
> *He's bigger than Godzilla or the monsters on TV;*
> *God is bigger than the Bogeyman,*
> *And He's watching out for you and me.*

Journal. I think things are going to get hot around here. I'm convinced now that we're about to encounter some spiritual warfare on the home turf. I've prayed God's protection and guidance over this household, and I know God's hand is in this place. Thank You, Lord Jesus, that Satan is a defeated foe.

The next day I knew why God laid it on several people's hearts to cover me in prayer. I was in Minna's new apartment helping her lay shelf paper in her tiny kitchen, when James came out. He stood in the doorway blocking my escape route and calmly observed, "You know I could just do that to you (and here he mimed placing his large hands around my neck and snapping it) and nobody would ever know."

I knew I was trapped. What could I do? I wondered how long it would be before they found my body. I asked him, "And why don't you do it?"

"I'm not allowed to," he said, "because of that big man in white standing behind you."

In great relief, joy, and tender compassion for his pain, I returned to my job at hand, thankful for God's angel of protection over me. Once again, I had received confirmation that God's loving hand had planned and orchestrated this whole bizarre journey.

On September 16, 2001, I got this message from little Timmy. I didn't know what to say.

> Dear Miss Karen,
>   Why is James so naughty? I don't like what he is saying. He is talking like Mrs. T. It makes me sad and angry. Should I talk to him and ask him why he is sad? Would that make him angry? I don't want him to be angry. Maybe he needs someone to hold him and let him cry. He needs someone to love him and give him happy feelings. It makes him sadder when he does bad things. He knows it makes a yucky feeling inside. I think he needs an inside bath to make him feel better. Then all the bad paintings will be washed away and he can draw nice paintings and have nice smells too. He makes me think about the hardness in my tummy. I don't want to think about that. I want to think about playing nice games and helping other people. He makes Amzie feel bad. He kept Minna and Amzie from sleeping last night and they are very tired. They don't want to sleep because they are worried that James will be bad when they can't do anything to stop it. How can I help them to sleep and not hear James? I tried to sing to him and he got mad 'cause he was scared. What should I do now?
>   timmy

Minna

I hated the thought of moving into my own apartment because I feared that everything would go back to the way it used to be, and I did not want to go back into the bondage from which I had so far escaped. I did not yet fully understand that the freedom I had gained was God-given and would not disappear just because I was out from under the direct influence of Karen and her effective prayers. When God gives freedom from lies experientially in the root memories, the lies cannot ever return. The mind is renewed in that place.

I've always had issues with feelings of abandonment. I first experienced this at birth when dad had to set me aside to take care of my mom as she hemorrhaged. Mom says when I cried out, she thought, "Who will take care of my little girl?" and her spirit remained.

Mom left me as an infant alone in my crib while she went across the compound to her teaching job. (At the time, my dad did not trust anyone to take care of me.) I could not escape the totally screened-in crib, which served to keep out the bugs, snakes, and rats. But while my parents were away, our gardener had access to me. And later still, my African caregiver would, under duress, take me to visit her witch doctor.

Besides the abuse (and perhaps because the abuse opened spiritual doors to demonic influence), I experienced other physical challenges over the years: cholera, thyroid issues, a broken neck in a car accident, and a depressed immune system. I've had fibromyalgia for as long as I can remember with resulting sores that cycle through my body. I believed that Satan had targeted me for destruction. But two things kept me alive and told me that someone wanted me. They helped me understand on some level that I wasn't being thrown away and that God loved me. First, I knew my parents wanted me. They had named me Minna Joy Kayser (Beloved Joy of the King of Kings). And I held onto one strong memory of my dad dancing with me at a very early age, twirling me around, eyes locked with mine.

CHAPTER FIFTEEN

Karen

Minna often tagged along when I went grocery shopping since she seemed incapable of making food decisions on her own. We'd drive to Wal-Mart, park our cars, and meet inside the store. It wouldn't take long before some Little Ones popped out and trailed behind me like a little kid in a candy shop. Everything fascinated them. I suppose the variety of merchandise was a little overwhelming to a child raised in an African village. I sometimes wondered what the other customers thought of this unlikely pair of shoppers, but I had to set aside my concerns and act like all was normal. After switching several times, when we emerged from the store with our purchases, another Alter would pop out who couldn't recall where they'd parked their car.

September 16, 2001. I remember the first time I met an infant personality. I did not know it was possible for a human to remember that far back, but when the trauma is severe and the personality splits, the baby is encapsulated in the memory. Since a baby cannot talk, how would I call out its name, reason with it, or explain that she needed to go into the memory? Not to worry. God had that covered. Another personality spoke for her and told me the baby was there. I simply prayed and asked the Lord how He wanted to minister to the baby. "He's rocking the baby and one of the children is singing to her 'Safe in the arms of Jesus' and she feels better now," the helper reported.

"Oh!" is all I could exclaim. Once more God confirmed that this process was not about me, but all about His amazing creation. Suddenly this children's song held special meaning:

Jesus loves me! This I know,
For the Bible tells me so.
Little Ones *to Him belong;*
They are weak, but He is strong.

After Minna started working, I received emails from some new personalities. It seems that each new environment or experience triggered another emotion and their accompanying memories. By this time, I'd begun using a notebook to keep track of all our conversations. On September 21, 2001, I heard from "Cain."

Hi Karen,
   I watch and see how you are little by little getting rid of us. That is not a very good thing to do. I am content with my life and do not want to go. I like what I feel and want to keep it the way it is.
   Cain

Thank you, Cain, for writing to me. What are you afraid of?

I am afraid of death and rejection.

Tell me about the times you've felt rejected.

I have always felt rejected by my family. They don't believe I exist and they don't want to believe it. I have come to the place where I don't want them to know now. I am rejected by society and I am an outcast in life.

What is your twin's name, by the way?

I am alone. I am a twin without a twin. This distress is mine alone to bear. Even Minna does not share this one with me. My destiny is to walk alone and to be rejected by all, then, to die alone as well.
   Cain

The next day, "Garth" wrote to me.

Hi Karen,
   You don't know me, but I have been paying attention to you. I would like to get together with you some time to talk. You sound like

*you have found some answers that I have been searching for. I want
to get rid of a heavy burden. Do you think you can help me?*
    Garth

Hi Garth,
    Thank you SO much for writing to me. Yes, I very much want to
get together to talk as soon as we can. Meanwhile, you can help me
by telling me your story or memory that you are holding. That will give
me a head start on understanding what you're feeling. How old were
you when you were traumatized?
    I'm also trying to get a handle on who all is related to whom, how
old each person is, who the helpers are, etc. If you can help me sort
out the groupings of the personalities, that would mean a lot.
    I look forward to meeting you.
    Karen

    *I was very young, but old enough to know that what was
happening was wrong. Possibly 3-4. I cannot help you much as I do
not pay attention to who is on the inside. I am more concerned with
the outside world. Though I am often reminded that I have children
to watch out for. Grace* [his twin] *can be quite a nag about that.
She doesn't like to have to watch hers and mine at the same time. I
tell her to relax since they are not going anywhere. Show me what
you have and I may be able to fill in some blanks. I don't know how
much I can help though. Grace is the one who usually keeps track
of everyone. If she feels like talking she might be helpful. She might
surprise you though. She is deaf. But she can do a lot of things
anyway.*
    Garth

On October 6, 2001, I heard again from Amzie.

Hi Karen,
    *I have been thinking a lot in the night and listening to Minna
praying. I feel like I am interfering with her life and progress spiritually.
She wants so much to be whole. But how can she find wholeness if
I am here as a constant reminder that she is different and can never
really have a normal life.*
    *I don't feel like I have a place or that I belong here. I just exist, am
in the way, and complicate things. I wish I could go and leave Minna
with peace and some semblance of a life. I have worked through a lot
of things, but this one still bothers me a lot.*
    *You are the only one who believes that I exist or who would
choose to believe. What good am I to Minna or anyone else? I feel*

like I come from another planet or am living in some kind of twilight zone. Am I really real? No one can answer that.

Which philosopher said "I think, therefore I am"? That is what I hang on to. I think. I feel. I have a drive to accomplish things in life. But then, so did the other personalities. So who am I? What am I? And do I belong here? . . . Or is it coming time for me to leave and I am fighting for my life like all the others?

I know I am rambling, but I have doubts. It would be so much easier to answer these things if I had my own body and could just look in the mirror. Who am I, Karen? You know me better than anyone. Why do I have to struggle with this? Will I ever find a place for myself that does not hinder Minna? I am just in the way!!

ARG

On October 25 I recorded: "Minna's healing is complete; the last of the personalities have integrated." Again we laugh. No one is completely healed till we get to heaven. Every other time a set of personalities integrated, she said she felt empty. This time she said, "I feel filled!" The first of the five sets took two and a half months to process as we built a trust relationship. The second set took eighteen hours, and the third to fifth sets took five hours. Once the facets of the diamond started to crack and crumble, the connecting points disintegrated. It amazed me to watch it happen. She told me when it was over that she had once prayed for a friend she could trust, but that friend had to be strong. I thank the Lord for that streak of stubbornness my mother often observed in me as a child. God placed that bulldog in my heart, but it had to be tamed.

Minna

He heals the brokenhearted and binds up their wounds (Psalm 147:3 NASB).

One day we sat down at Karen's kitchen table to list some of the changes I had experienced in the past few months.

No more compulsive removing of labels
No more compulsive hand washing
No more feelings of guilt, shame, abandonment, etc.

I can rest now
No more blackouts
No more fear of spiders
My number of migraines greatly reduced
No more self-mutilation
No more stuttering
I feel hunger for the first time!
No longer viewing females as "attainable / unattainable"
Having hair in my face feels ok now
No longer need for extreme order
No more suicidal thoughts

Some of the truths God gave me:

I feel clean.
Jesus is giving me a bath—like a bucket of water thrown over me.
He's holding me.
I'm not scared anymore.
I'm safe.
The man won't hurt me anymore.
I'm floating on a cloud.
There's only calm. He touched the water and it's peaceful.
The bad pictures don't bother me anymore.
The pain is gone!
He loves me.
It's not my fault.
I'm not guilty. I don't feel ashamed anymore.

I remember what it felt like to experience tears for the first time. When I first arrived on Karen's doorstep, my face revealed no affect — my emotions locked down tight. But after enough healing had taken place, a little bit of grief surfaced. I was astounded. *I'm leaking! What's happening?* And I tried to stop it because it felt inappropriate. Crying at boarding school, after all, was a sign of weakness to my peers. I remember the adults who told me there was no reason to cry and not to feel so deeply. Keeping one's emotions under control meant survival. Now at last I found myself in a safe place where I could begin to mourn my losses.

CHAPTER SIXTEEN

Karen

Though we were experiencing great success, there came a point in our processing where we needed more information and training. We knew we lacked something in our understanding of D.I.D. And so with our Mission's blessing and support, we flew to California on November 28 to attend the Advanced Seminar in the inner healing prayer ministry training.

First we learned about working with people who had phobias, addictions, and compulsions (such as drinking, gambling, pornography, eating disorders, and cutting). I began to grasp the concept that the outward behavior is merely the coping mechanism for handling the inner pain. Using inner healing prayer is an effective tool for getting quickly to the root of the problem and receiving truth from the Lord, with the result that the coping mechanism is no longer needed. Simple. Got that. . . . Next? Next we learned about how to work with multiples. Since that's what we'd been doing all along, it now felt comfortable and familiar.

With Minna as my teacher, I had learned much about D.I.D. A split in the personality occurs most often in early childhood as a result of repetitive, often torturous, sexual or physical abuse. Dissociation is more prevalent in girls than in boys. Some people split into just two or three simple parts; others are very complex and numerous, depending on the severity of the abuse. And every person splits in a unique way. A child may name her parts using ordinary, mythical, celebrity, or even plant and animal names. Apparently some people who are dissociated have a total amnesiac wall to their personalities (that's Minna) while others are co-conscious with, or aware of, their other parts. Most cases of D.I.D. are not diagnosed until adulthood. This sounded more and more complicated, but I'd already experienced the Holy Spirit's leading every step of the way, so I knew we could do this.

Each time Minna's personalities had presented, I had recorded their names and ages, what the issue was, what lies they believed, and what truth God told them before they integrated. (Not every person with D.I.D. names their parts, by the way.) I could call parts out just by using their names (if they were willing). Some of the parts, I had learned, wrote left-handed, some with their right. Some wrote backwards, some slanting one way, some another. Each had his/her own voice quality (it was very obvious that some were children or babies when they were "out") with different and distinct personality traits. Some were mute, others were deaf, and I had even encountered a few that were blind—a result of the type of trauma they experienced. When told, for example, that they would die if they told the secret, they took a vow of silence. Others might have been blindfolded in the memory and were incapable of seeing what took place. Sometimes an especially traumatic memory split into multiple parts where one part held the trauma of the sounds, another of the physical pain, and another of the visual aspect of the same memory. Because Minna had lived overseas, some of her parts only spoke Amharic or German.

In each case, God had given us the answer we needed at just the right time to be able to communicate. For the foreign languages, I would write down the words phonetically and then call Minna out to listen and interpret for us. She had some good laughs at my pronunciation. For mute ones who were too young to write, they drew pictures and I guessed a lot. A couple times a mutual friend happened to be present who knew sign language and interpreted for us. It had been an amazing journey of faith for us so far.

We learned at the seminar that integration was not to be our goal. Integration is simply a by-product of the healing process. Neither was it to be our objective to prove or disprove that an event had occurred. That helped put my mind at ease. Memories are simply the containers for the lies, and every person remembers things differently and from

meine name ist Heinrich (20)
meine freundin also
wie alt bist du? 48
Ich bin 20 jahre alt

Das ist meine lieblingsbuche
Es ist meine geschichte

Es war nicht gut. Es war so
evil
hungerich für alles möglich sex
meine oglich cusina laughlich
Ich kann nicht sagen
Sie saght das ich kann nicht diese
langen sagen trochen.

Translation:
My name is Heinrich
My girlfriend also
    [I don't remember the question I asked him.]
How old are you?
    [Karen – 48]
I am 20 years old.
This is my favorite book.
    [We must have discussed a book title?]
It is my story.
It was not good. It was so evil.
I hunger for all possible sex.
    [Not sure of next line]
I cannot say.
I can't say anything about this to anyone.

his or her own perspective. Memories are fluid and can be changed over time by later events and interpretations. Rather it is important to identify what the person believes during or after the memory occurs. Once God replaces the lies with His truth, the emotions in the memory calm down. The memory doesn't go away: it is what it is. But there will only be peace and calm when the victim looks back at the pictures in his or her mind. Our goal is to bring all pain to the feet of the Lord Jesus. Once the pain is gone, the need for revenge goes away, and forgiveness becomes easier. Often a victim will then feel sad for the abuser, and God can minister even to that sadness.

People sometimes confuse forgiveness with reconciliation. Forgiveness is a choice by one person; reconciliation is a choice by two people. Forgiveness frees the abused, but reconciliation is only possible if both abuser and victim agree to a restored relationship. If the abuser is deceased, then reconciliation is obviously impossible. Thankfully, forgiveness is not contingent on the abuser offering an apology.

Minna had been admonished by some to "forget what is behind," quoting from Philippians 3:13-14. But as we studied the context of the passage, we discovered that "the past" referred to the Apostle Paul's past accomplishments, not his past pain. *If anyone else thinks he has reasons to put confidence in the flesh, I have more: circumcised on the eighth day, of the people of Israel, of the tribe of Benjamin, a Hebrew of Hebrews; in regard to the law, a Pharisee; as for zeal, persecuting the church; as for legalistic righteousness, faultless. But whatever was to my profit I now consider loss for the sake of Christ (Philippians 3:4b-7 NIV).* It's impossible to put the past behind you when it's always in front of you. Only when inner healing occurs is it possible to move forward.

The missing piece to the diamond fractal fell into place for me when the seminar speaker explained that there could be three different layers or types of personalities. The first is a child part (what we had been calling the Little One). This is the part that experienced the original trauma and is caught in the memory in a sort of time-warp. He/she will always be the same age if you talk to him/her. For example, when I met seven-year-old Randi, he declared that it was raining outside. I knew that wasn't true at that moment in 2001, but it was reality to him because he was actually living the memory as we spoke. When he said he was "afraid of the bad men" I tried to tell him "There are no bad men. You're safe here." I didn't understand that he was actually in the moment, experiencing the event. We learned that there will be no true and lasting healing until the Little One hears truth from Jesus, and He takes away his pain.

The second layer can be called a "Helper," "Protector," "Guardian," or "Alter." The mind creates this part to protect the Little Ones inside. The Guardian is often birthed at the time of the child's trauma and can grow in maturity. Thus, if I asked him (or her) how old he was, he might say he was 47 (when in actuality, the body — aka Minna — had been born 53 years ago). Dani and Michael were Guardians. To my great relief, I learned that each of these Alters did not need to be saved. They were simply doing their job of keeping the child from feeling more pain. Once the child's pain is removed, their protective job is done, and they can integrate. Sometimes helpers balk at the idea of losing their job, but God often affirms that He has a new job for them to do.

The final layer seems to be the core child — the original person God created who got stunted in mental and emotional growth due to the trauma. More about that later . . .

We began to see how D.I.D. is not a disorder at all, but rather very orderly. An Alter System is truly ingenious. In His grace, God provides a way of coping when the physical or emotional pain is too great. Later, when the victim's brain begins to tire of the coping mechanism that's in place, it will begin to leak information or emotion that before it had locked away tight. Emotions out of synch with normal events, flashbacks, and acts of attempted self-destruction are all clues that something bad happened in their past. The adult mind is more capable of handling the truth, and healing can now begin as the person chooses to turn and face his pain instead of escape from it.

Dissociation, we learned, can happen on a continuum from mild to severe. In a minor way, we all dissociate to some degree from life's events. I did this a lot during boring classes — my mind would wander in the great outdoors while the teacher droned on and on about historical dates and events. When I came back to reality, I may or may not remember a thing the teacher said. My body may have been there, but my mind provided a way of escape. The child that is traumatized often dissociates as well. She thinks about something else during the event so she can tolerate the pain of the moment. This is not mere daydreaming, however, but some sort of actual split or compartmentalization in the brain. The difference is that once her mind comes back to reality, she cannot remember having been physically there experiencing the trauma. The memory is safely locked away in a separate section of the brain. It's not a chemical imbalance, a genetic deformity, or even an aberration. It is one normal way for the brain to cope with pain.

What's interesting to me is how, after working with Minna, I'd grown accustomed to the bizarre. Some things sound bizarre to us because we've not been exposed to them before. Some things are bizarre because in a group of 100, only 1 person exhibits a particular characteristic. But in a large group of D.I.D. individuals, their behavior would all be normal for them. I found out how common this phenomenon actually is.

The last part of our seminar dealt with the topic of S.R.A. (Satanic Ritual Abuse). The information came at me deep and fast and overwhelming. The whole concept was new to me, so the learning curve was quite steep. Not every D.I.D. is an S.R.A. victim, but every S.R.A. victim dissociates. Our speaker said that if normal or common D.I.D. can be measured on a scale of 1-25 (with 25 being the most severe), then S.R.A. victims START at 800 and go off the charts. *What did he mean by that*? I wondered. He talked about false realities and programming and mind control. My head was spinning. At the end of that day's training session, I turned to Minna and exclaimed, "Whew! I'm so glad you're not an S.R.A. victim. I don't think I could handle that!"

My heart sank when she looked at me, hesitated, and then responded, "I don't know, Karen. This sounds awfully familiar to me." I looked at her in disbelief. Minna has a degree in psychology, so I figured she'd studied this at some point. But that was not the real source of her knowledge. Her parts inside knew the truth because they'd experienced it. And so we trudged into another beginning.

Minna

When the speaker began to introduce the topic of S.R.A., I started seeing pictures in my mind . . . *too familiar . . . no way! . . . I don't want it to be that.* I balked at it inside. And I heard a voice inside say, "Tough luck!"

Now what! This felt both scary and discouraging. But I saw events that were beyond what I had seen before. Someone inside showed me just a little snapshot of what had happened. I could feel their excitement that maybe now they could finally find safety in telling their secrets and find relief from the pain.

Karen

Minna and I returned home, and our processing began to peel back the layers of S.R.A. memories. The seminar speaker had warned us, "Do not take on an S.R.A. victim unless God TELLS you to." Well, I guess God had already told me to, so off we went. Every time an issue arose, we'd get together and pray through it. He also warned us never to plant a victory stake, thinking that full integration had occurred. I tried to remember his warning.

The details of S.R.A. stories are best left to the imagination—unless you find yourself working with a victim—in which case, extensive training is highly recommended. By way of summary, S.R.A. is a form of mind control in which the victim is subjected to unimaginable torture, rape, and abuse. Everything sacred in the kingdom of God is perverted and desecrated by Satan and his minions. Origins of this idolatry can be found in the Scriptures where God severely condemns the offering of children on the altars of Baal. S.R.A. is practiced covertly the world over (including in secret societies such as the Masons), but in Africa it was openly rampant in the villages with local witch doctors.

Some people question the veracity of a victim's stories. The events sound just too horrific and implausible. But the therapist (or friend) who dismisses a story with "That's impossible" will soon lose the victim's trust and willingness to open up. The abuser has repeatedly told the victim that no one will believe her. Right from the beginning, no matter how incredible or bizarre the tale, I assured Minna that I did believe her. I knew that I could never prove that a particular event had or had not happened, but her behavior convinced me that something really bad had happened to her. Was it just her perception of an event like a witness at an auto accident? Would another witness claim it hadn't happened that way? Our goal was not to prove or disprove, but simply to replace lies with truth and come to a place of peace instead of pain in each memory that surfaced.

However, any doubts I had that she was telling the truth dissipated after hearing independent, corroborating stories from other AMKs who had experienced the same events and named the same abusers. What surprised me the most (and further convinced me of the veracity of her stories) was watching her abreaction (the involuntary acting out of symptoms in the body). When in a choking memory, for instance, Minna's neck would turn bright red. When a knife memory surfaced, the scar would welt up. One day we were working through a memory when she had the mumps, and I watched in fascination as her neck began to swell to twice its normal size. It doesn't take much imagination to figure out what's going on in a memory when the person is writhing in agony. While reliving the memory, every cell in the body remembers the pain until the person receives truth, and then the body can calm down with a sense of peace. It's a mind-boggling, fascinating thing to watch God heal the mind as well as the body.

I learned I had to build relationships with the Alters or Guardians. They had to know I was trustworthy and would not harm the Little Ones they were protecting. Once it felt safe, they'd let a Little One out, but then I'd have get to know that one as well. One of the ways I was able to win over Minna's Little Ones was to tell them stories. They were often hesitant to go into the memory – either because it was too painful or they were told not to tell on threat of punishment or death. They had made vows that they were not willing to break. Many times I'd find myself making up a story that had just the right element in it that touched on their issue. Only the Holy Spirit could have orchestrated those thoughts.

Minna

I didn't know how bizarre my life was. This was my normal. I could sense what people were feeling, but I didn't know what they were thinking of me. Sometimes I would make what I thought was a mild comment about something I'd experienced, and they'd respond with shock or disbelief. Or they'd say I shared too much . . . I went too deep too fast, and it would scare them off.

I will spare you the details of the horror and torture my abusers subjected me to, but perhaps one example will give you an understanding of why a child turns from God as a result of her experiences. During a rape and beating, the abusers might tell the child to call on Jesus to save her. When she obeys, one of two things can happen. When Jesus doesn't show up, they tell her, "See, he doesn't want you and you'll never get to heaven." Or . . . a person named "Jesus" shows up dressed in white robes and tells the child, "You're not worth saving," and then he walks away. The lie is forever implanted in the child's mind until the True Lord Jesus whispers in her heart, "I want you. You're precious. I will never leave you or forsake you." If the child responds, "But You weren't there when I needed you!" Jesus might answer, "I was there. I saw it all."

One preschool memory stands out in my mind of God's protection over me during the rituals. One day I was taken by the hand, and we came up to a cave on the mountain behind our station. The abusers instructed me, "We're going to cover you in butter, and you're going to walk through the snake pit. If Satan accepts you, the snakes will lick you and you'll come out the other side safe and sound."

I refused to do it. My daddy had taught me that I shouldn't do something for Satan. But then they told me, "If you don't do it, we'll have to kill your daddy and then all the Africans will go to hell because they won't hear his preaching, and it will be all your fault."

I was scared to go through the snake pit because I knew I would die. I knew Satan wouldn't choose me because I belonged to God. I was in a double bind. If I did this, it was wrong; if I did that, it was wrong. I concluded that it was better for me to die because I knew I was going to heaven, and I didn't want to be responsible for the deaths of all those Africans.

And so they covered me in butter, and I crawled into the pit. As I inched my way forward, I saw a shining man in white clothes who showed me the way through the pit to the other side to safety.

God has a purpose for my life. He allowed me to suffer indescribable pain, but He always rescued me from death. Satan could only touch me so far and no farther.

Karen

Journal, December 10, 2001. How long has it been since I read Ezekiel!? Chapter one is like fresh manna to me. A glimpse into the world of the unseen, the heavenlies — the wonder, the beauty. I've been given a tiny glimpse into the world of the occult through our seminar on S.R.A. victims. And I've been given a taste for the spirit world through my work with M. Three times her personalities have mentioned seeing an angel about me, and three times I've encountered demonic activity.

Ezekiel 21. One thing I'm learning through inner healing prayer is that God's sovereignty is over all wickedness and evil. He uses Satan (in the sense that one uses an instrument to accomplish one's purpose.) God is not up in heaven wringing His hands every time Satan "triumphs." He not only turns Satan's schemes around for good, but He actually USES Satan to accomplish His purposes. Wow!

CHAPTER SEVENTEEN

Karen

People often ask me how my family coped with this enormous intrusion in our family life. Our oldest daughter (19) focused on working and spending time with her church friends, knowing that she only had a couple months before returning to college. She told me later that there was something about Minna that she didn't trust, but she never felt afraid. Mostly they stayed out of each other's way. Our middle daughter (17) kept busy with her senior year in high school, and I worried that she might feel neglected due to all the intensive hours I spent with Minna—who always seemed to be in the midst of a crisis. She said God gave her the understanding that "Minna needed you more than I did." My youngest daughter (13) was a real trooper. She adored Minna and all her Little Ones. They felt comfortable around her and sometimes they related better to her than to me.

But my husband struggled. He wasn't convinced at this point that inner healing prayer was a viable form of therapy, and I'm sure he often felt like I'd gone off the deep end in this newfound passion of mine. He understood and accepted the deep bond of friendships I had with other MKs, but this MK was a little too far out in left field for his taste. By this time I'd explained to him about Minna's dissociation, but he didn't quite get it. Generally, Minna tried to keep her distance from him. But one time one of her Alters felt triggered by something Scott said and challenged him. Scott did not take kindly to her tone and was ready to kick Minna out of the house. When I conveyed that to Minna, she was horrified. "I didn't say that!" she insisted. And that's when we realized it had been an angry Alter who was out. Quickly I explained the situation to Scott, and he felt relieved. He just knew that was not the normal tone he heard from Minna. This incident opened his eyes at last to D.I.D.

And so Minna wrote him a letter.

Minna

December 15, 2001

Dear Scott,

I don't want to go home [for Christmas] without letting you know how grateful I am that you have been both generous and gracious toward me in the last 5 ½ months, as I have spent so much time with Karen going through an incredible journey.

In the months I have spent with your family, I have learned so much. God has led me back to the past where He has brought healing and great joy and peace to me, which I had not been able to find before. When I came into your life I was a wounded MK who could not get my life together no matter how I tried. I had only planned to stay and visit for a few days. As you know, I ended up getting stuck and needing a job because my savings were depleted. As I look back on it I can see the Hand of God orchestrating my circumstances so that I could no longer avoid the painful memories I was trying to forget. I am so glad Karen was faithful in helping me to face the issues that I needed to deal with. I know I have a very long way to go when measured against a standard of perfection. I am grateful that God doesn't demand perfection.

Karen helped me go back into memories that held pain, and we identified the lies that I believed and asked the Lord to show me the truth. He was faithful to share His truth, and when He did, the pain was replaced with peace in each memory we addressed. This has given me a deeper understanding of what was meant by, "the truth shall set you free." I didn't realize just how bound I was as a prisoner of the past until I experienced the freeing power of God's truth. I knew the truth in my head, but I had not experienced it in my heart where the wounding lies held me captive. Jesus "sets the captive free" when He experientially shares The Truth.

This probably doesn't make a whole lot of sense to you. The only way I know how to share what I have experienced is to share some of what I have been released from.

I was abused and molested repeatedly throughout my childhood by a number of people. When the abuse started, I was too young to make much sense out of it. God has promised that He will not give us more than we can bear but will make a way of escape. He gave my young mind a way to create order in the chaos of my environment. He created a safety feature in the mind to preserve sanity. That safety feature is the ability to separate from what is happening through dissociation. The conscious mind secures the memory in the subconscious mind so that a person can function. How this manifests varies from person to person and is dependent on the age at which the abuse starts, the severity of the abuse, and often the nature of the abuse. Some people have memories that are locked away through straightforward amnesia. Other people split into protector personalities who bear the abuse. The child then does not remember what happened and carries on with life, but the memories are carried by a personality whose purpose is to remember for the child and to bear the pain of those memories.

The trouble with dissociation is that even though you do not remember the trauma, the effects leak out eventually and color every aspect of your conscious life. At some point in time you have to face the memories and deal with them.

I have shared all of that because I am excited by what God is doing in my life. I want to thank you for being part of the process with your kindness to me. I look forward to the future now with joy and expectation because I know God is not finished with me yet. If He were finished with me, I would be perfect and we both know I am not. ☺

Minna

CHAPTER EIGHTEEN

Karen

During that whole first year, I thought God had brought Minna to my doorstep so I could help bring healing to her troubled past. It never occurred to me at the time that God had brought her in answer to my own prayers for healing. I had been struggling with my own secret for years before Minna came into my life. I had cried out to God to give me an answer, but He seemed silent.

One day Minna and I were strolling by a stream when one of her Little Ones popped out. When I tried to pray with him, he challenged me. "Miss Karen, I've been watching you work with the others inside," he said, "but I don't really believe it will work for me."

"What would convince you?" I asked.

"First I want to see YOU process YOUR stuff," he replied.

I was stumped. I didn't know what he meant. I never once struggled with doubts about my salvation. I had never been abused; I had godly parents who loved me; I enjoyed my years at boarding school—what did I have to work on?

"Ask Minna," he suggested. So, I called Minna's name, and she switched back out. I told her what her Little One had said, and she laughed.

"Yes, you do have some issues," she said. "I've been watching you."

"Like what?"

"How about what you're feeling about raising your three girls?" she replied.

Gulp. She was right. I was worried about their future and how God would provide for them in college. And so, as I'd instructed Minna many times over, I focused on my emotions. I knew that once I actually felt the fear, my mind should automatically take me to the source and origin of that fear because emotion is the bridge to the past. If I had simply used logic to try to figure it out, I may have landed in a different memory. Once I was in the memory where I first experienced this kind of fear, Minna asked me why I felt afraid and what I believed about it. I admitted that I believed I was responsible for my girls' success in life, and I was afraid of failing them. Then Minna prayed and asked the Lord what truth He wanted me to know. God whispered in my mind and heart (not in an audible voice, but in an assurance of truth) that my girls belonged to Him, and that they were His responsibility. I had dedicated them to Him at birth after all. Wow! Immediately a sense of relief and peace came over me. The fear was gone! I opened my eyes and looked at Minna in astonishment. "Is this what you've been experiencing all this time?" I exclaimed. "You mean if I take care of the lies in my past, the present emotion will calm down in the present?"

I knew I wanted more. From then on, each time I recognized a negative emotion (and occasionally even a positive one that wasn't rooted in truth), I stopped and processed it. I had no idea I believed so many lies. Jesus had said, *Then you will know the truth, and the truth will set you free (John 8:32 NIV).* Now I knew it experientially. Often I would get stuck and would ask Minna to pray with me. Many times she was faithful to point out emotions I tried to ignore and challenged me to deal with them. What a gift God gave me to have a friend who wasn't afraid to confront!

Then the day came when I knew it was time to face my issue—the one I'd been holding secret in my heart for so long. I could feel the inner reluctance. Why was it so hard to talk about it? Minna had spent the last year trusting me with her innermost secrets and sharing the most intimate details imaginable, and I felt like a wimp admitting that I had just one little thing I needed to work on—not a big thing really. Nothing in comparison to what she'd been through. And besides, my problem was self-induced. At least hers was as a result of someone else's choices. But I wanted what she had — freedom from the guilt and shame.

And so I began. I admitted to her that I had been struggling with emotional affairs — infidelity of the heart. A physical affair was out of the question. I had strong boundaries in place against that. But God said that infidelity begins in the heart, and though I wanted no part of it, I couldn't seem to stop the emotions that accompanied them. I wanted to know the source and origin of the bondage in which I found myself. My mind went back to all past relationships with guys, and one by one I broke all emotional bonds with them. I was a virgin when I got married, but I recognized that I had spent my teen years trying to fill a hole in my heart.

And then I went a little deeper. I wanted to know how and why that hole got there in the first place. That's when I landed in a childhood memory — a little four- or five-year-old girl with her clothes off, play-acting with the little African boys. I didn't know at the time that what we were playing was merely an imitation of what they'd witnessed the grownups doing in their communal-living hut. But I knew in my heart that it felt secret and shameful — not something you'd want your mother to discover you doing, that's for sure. I had long ago asked God to forgive me — in fact, it was probably because of that guilt that I asked Jesus into my heart as a five-year-old. I knew He'd forgiven me, but the shame and dirty feelings never lifted — not until the day Minna prayed with me. I asked God to break the unholy bonds that were created in that scene, and then I saw myself clothed in white garments, cleansed, pure, forgiven, shame-free. Immediately I noticed a change in my heart. The hole was filled, and the tug toward emotional infidelity was gone — never to come back. I was free. I learned that day how powerful sexual bonds can be and why God is so adamant about purity.

Journal. I feel a deep-seated contentment right now. I'm beginning to catch a glimpse of what it feels like to sit at the feet of Jesus. Inner healing prayer has opened my eyes and understanding . . . it settles me down to hear God's sweet, gentle words of love and affirmation. I don't ever want to lose what I've learned over the past three months. Thank You, Father, for keeping my feet to the fire. . . . I have never felt more alive than I do today. Sweet fellowship. Sweet awareness of God's presence and His voice. I'm only now beginning to catch a glimpse into how some live by the Father's direction, moment by moment.

With my new-found freedom, my fix-it mentality kicked into high gear. With this effective tool at my disposal, I began to accost my family and friends. My antennae shot up whenever I sensed someone emoting, and soon everyone became weary with my incessant queries, "What are you feeling? What memory does that emotion belong to? Do you want to get rid of that pain?" Scott jokingly declared he would inscribe "How does that make you feel?" on my tombstone.

Minna

My spiritual journey could not have been a greater contrast to Karen's. Someone told me that at age five I asked Jesus into my heart. I never doubted God's existence, but because of my abuse, I struggled with seeing God as caring or interactive. I imagined Him as being up in heaven with a club in His hand ready to beat me if I did the slightest thing wrong. That's what boarding school had taught me. There was a time in my teen years when I thought to myself that I wanted to find my own faith and not live by my parents' faith. I didn't know how to do that, but I determined to try.

At age sixteen, I left my parents in Africa and flew to Toronto, Ontario, Canada. Because of an air strike in Germany, we were twelve hours late, and there was no one there to meet me at 3 a.m. I found a phone book, opened it up to a random page, pointed at a name, and thought, *That sounds like a missionary name.* I called the number, and it actually turned out to be one of our missionaries! He came and picked me up and took me to Mission headquarters. After two weeks there, I flew to Calgary, Alberta, where my uncle picked me up and took me to the boarding school at Prairie High. Somehow the money my parents sent to the Mission to cover my schooling expenses never reached me.

I felt alone in the world, but at least I was away from Mr. Ahab, my abuser. I got a job on campus and enrolled myself in school.

When I considered driving a truck, I heard someone say, "Women can't do that"; so immediately I went out and got an underage hardship license to prove that I could. Nobody was going to tell me I couldn't do something! I didn't know at the time that my reaction stemmed from Mr. Ahab's challenge, "You'll never amount to anything." And so I had to prove myself—and I got into lots of mischief.

After I graduated from high school, ten of my classmates decided to get an apartment together. We all worked different shifts, so we just rotated in and out of the space. Two of them were potheads, and so I decided to try some drugs. That night I drove ten miles and couldn't remember any part of the trip. That was the first and last time I indulged. I did not like being out of control. It was through one of my roomies that I first tried alcohol that actually tasted good.

I had started smoking at age nine in Canada when we were home on furlough. I got the cigarettes from a neighbor kid, and I got hooked. In Africa I rolled my own cigarettes straight out of the tobacco fields. I realized I was allergic to the smoke but I couldn't quit.

I entered Prairie Bible Institute and at age eighteen, through one of L.E. Maxwell's sermons, I made the decision as an adult to accept Christ. I really pursued God, but one day I deliberately walked away from Him when I met Patty. Why? Because she was "unattainable." I always had a hard time turning down a challenge. I knew that if I went after her, it would be like walking away from God. But I made that choice. I told God, aloud, that He could just get lost because I didn't like all the Pharisees around there. Every Christian around me seemed like a hypocrite.

I wanted to conquer and break her. She was straight-laced, straight-backed, prim-and-proper—a person trying to follow God (but not too successfully). Someone told me I was dirt class—that I was too low down to associate with someone at her high level. I recognized that she was living a lie, a Pharisee herself. In the process of the pursuit, I had worn her down enough that I could have done anything I wanted.

I wanted to have her. It was the quest, the conquest that drove me. I wanted to break her pride.

One day I took her out into a cornfield and I told her, "I'm going to have you, and there's nothing you can do about it." She was afraid, thinking I could have killed her and left her body there. But at the same time, she felt drawn to me, so she acquiesced, and I ended up having a lesbian relationship with her.

After this ten-year wild side, a woman approached me and asked if I was gay. I admitted to it, and she said she'd like to experience that. So I had a two-and-a-half-year relationship with her (dumb thing to do), but she made me mad and I left. I felt stupid. It was an experiment, not a relationship. I was always looking for something, but I had buried it down so deep I didn't know what it was. People rejected me so many times, I had to prove things.

When I got tired of being nagged by Patty, I decided I didn't want to take it anymore, and so I told her I didn't love her anymore. I left a broken heart behind. I was blunt—no gentleness or kindness. She was a used toy that I was bored with. I'd had enough fun. She was passive aggressive and I was just plain aggressive. I had become what I hated— an abuser.

After that, I got into all kinds of worldly activities. I drank heavily and smoked four packs of cigarettes a day. It was the only way I knew how to cope. My defense mechanisms started to break down, though, and life became more painful. The emotions started to leak out, but I didn't know the source of them. By now I'd enrolled in university pursuing a degree in psychology. Every night I would meet a friend at a restaurant to study and drink and smoke. But I never got drunk out of my mind. I never wanted to lose total control. In 1995, I spoke out loud, "Lord, I need to quit smoking, but I can't." I took another puff, got very sick, threw up, and quit on the spot never to start up again. Amazingly, He answered my prayer and I didn't even have a relationship with Him at the time.

During this time, I made myself so busy that I couldn't get into trouble, hoping that that would take the pain away. I worked three part-time jobs and was a student in two full-time programs in two separate universities. Always trying to kill the pain.

On July 3, 1997, my world screeched to a halt. I was in a car accident. I had had to stop suddenly on a busy road, and a truck carrying large electrical spools smashed into me, squashing my car so thoroughly that I popped out into oncoming traffic. I called my parents from the hospital to let them know what had happened and asked them to collect my stuff out of my car. They were afraid when they saw the wreckage, wondering how badly I'd been hurt. I'd damaged my wrist, shoulder, lower back, and ribs. I couldn't walk well for a long time, and I discovered that when I'd hit my head, I'd permanently damaged the left side of my brain. I was forty years old, and God had started to get my attention . . . for I felt more than just physical pain.

That's when God told me, "I want you." How ironic that He would want me when I was all damaged and broken!

Graduation from UBC in 1999 with a BA in
Psychology

CHAPTER NINETEEN

Karen

[We] thank Christ Jesus our Lord, who has given [us] strength, that he considered [us] faithful, appointing [us] to his service (1 Timothy 1:12 NIV).

About this time, we sensed the Lord calling us to work with other struggling AMKs (Adult Missionary Kids). We realized that God had brought us to this point for a purpose. He never wastes our pain. And so we began to ask the Lord to show us what to do. We determined we would not go seeking out people, but would trust that He would bring to us only what we could handle. We called ourselves M&K Ministry (with the double allusion to Minna & Karen or Missionary Kids). And we solicited prayer support from fifty individuals who committed to pray regularly for us and our ministry.

Anne was our first "ministeree." While Minna was home for Christmas, she had made the effort to connect with a boarding school dorm mate who lived nearby. She shared with Anne what she'd been learning and urged her to seek healing as well. Minna knew that Anne was also a victim of Mr. Ahab's torture, but she wisely kept quiet about his identity. Anne needed to identify him from her own memory bank. She wanted to know more about how to get rid of her pain, and so we invited her to come to Tennessee for an intensive time of prayer together.

Slowly God began to bring more people to our doorstep for ministry. One person would tell another, and soon we were booked with appointments to meet with hurting people in our community. We were still on our own healing journey, but we decided we couldn't wait till we were completely whole — whatever that meant — before we could be used of God.

We discovered that different people processed their memories and emotions in different ways, and God ministered to them according to how their minds worked. Some people "heard" from God (thoughts in their minds or, more rarely, in an audible voice). Some saw pictures in their minds (for example, they'd report seeing Jesus walking toward them). Some experienced Him physically. (They felt the warmth of His presence or the removal of the pain associated with memories.)

After being stuck for a long time with one person, we happened to discover what we now term the "symbolic processor." This is the person who needs a visual representation or symbol for their emotion. For example "fear" to this person might be represented by a dog snarling. Or anger is like a flame of fire. Surprisingly, I realized that I processed best this way as well. The challenge (and fun) of meeting new people was learning how their minds worked and then applying basic inner healing prayer principles.

Early on in our ministry, we experienced a lot of demonic interference. It always seemed to happen just as the person began to really feel the pain and was on the verge of hearing truth from the Lord. The phone would ring, someone would knock on the door, or there'd be some other distraction. One day we were in the middle of processing with a lady in my living room when suddenly my car started honking all by itself in the garage. Starting and stopping the engine made no difference. Thankfully, Minna knew how to disable the horn. By that time, the mood in the room had drastically changed. That's when we began to pray against demonic interruptions and interference BEFORE we began each session. The number of incidents dramatically dropped after that.

We began to sit up and take notice if there was an interruption. We knew it was often an indication that we were on the right track. One morning we were meeting with a lady in one of the rooms in the children's wing of our church. We were feeling stuck and uncertain what direction to go. Just then a group of preschoolers from the daycare came into the hallway, causing some distraction to our focus.

We stopped and prayed that God would remove the distraction for us. Nothing happened. The children remained outside the door, talking and laughing. I could feel my frustration rising when suddenly one of the children kicked our door. I assumed there was a strong demonic presence out there. Just then the lady looked up and exclaimed, "That's it! That kick reminded me of a memory," and she was able to go right to the place that would get her unstuck. We learned that day that God can use any means at His disposal to accomplish His purpose.

We were always dependent on listening to the Holy Spirit when we prayed. One time when I was praying with Minna, she started to perform a repetitive motion. She had been programmed by her perpetrators to act in certain ways to prevent her from entering into the memories. I knew that if I held her hands still, I could expedite the process. But my strength was no match for Minna's. The Little One would simply toss me aside and keep up the action. The Lord prompted me to pray for an angel to hold her hands still. I watched in amazement as her action stopped and she was able to enter into the painful place.

When we first began praying with people who were multiple, we'd sometimes find strong Guardian Alters in place, and it would take a while to gain their trust before they'd let us get near the Little Ones they were protecting. One day we were getting to know some resistant Alters of an S.R.A. victim, and we felt stumped. And so we paused and waited, praying for some insight. I glanced around the room and noticed my daughter's art project in the corner. She'd created an egg in a nest with a little fairy sitting on top of the egg. The Holy Spirit gave me the idea to talk about it. I explained to the Alter that he was like the fairy, guarding something very precious inside, and we were not here to harm the Little One. We just wanted permission to talk to her, but that we would like for him to stay really close by and watch to make sure she was okay. And that, if we did or said anything that made him uncomfortable, he could step in and protect her again. That seemed to satisfy him, and he let us proceed.

Sometimes God made appointments for us that weren't penciled into the calendar. One day I had a lot of errands to run, and as I thought through the best route to take for the greatest efficiency and gas consumption, Wal-Mart came up first on my list. I parked the car, grabbed a cart, and "accidentally" met one of our S.R.A. victims coming out of the store. The look on her face was priceless, as she exclaimed, "I just prayed ten to fifteen minutes ago: Lord, I need to see Karen or Minna right now!" She was in crisis mode as she was on her way to a family member's funeral. And so God's business was done in a makeshift office (her air-conditioned car in Wal-Mart's parking lot) as we prayed together and she released her panic and dread to the Great Physician. "God is so good" she kept reiterating. Indeed He is! Later she reported, "The funeral was amazing! No terror or panic. Just peace. I cannot thank you enough for following the leading of God and being there. I don't know what I would have done." There are truly no words to describe the love, mercy, and grace of our Father in heaven.

Another day, I walked into the dental office a few minutes early and sat down in the waiting room. Immediately, the only other person in the room (an African-American man) turned to me and said, "I hate being here. I've served in the military and I've jumped out of airplanes, but I'm scared of a little ol' dental appointment." Sensing his nervousness, I asked, "Why are you so fearful of it?"

Pause. "I'll tell you why," he replied. "When I was a little boy, my father had to wear dentures, and I remember the awful pain he had to go through."

"Why was that so fearful to you?" I asked again.

He thought a moment. "Because I could imagine the tools the dentist had to use to extract his teeth."

"What were you imagining?" I asked.

"A chisel and a screwdriver."

And so I asked him gently, "Would you like me to pray with you?"

His eyes lit up, he grabbed my hands, and exclaimed, "Sure!"

"Just look at the picture of the tools and focus on the fear," I told him. And then I prayed, "Lord, what do You want to show this man in that picture?"

Immediately he relaxed. "He took them [the tools] away!"

115

"And how's the fear now?"

"It's gone! Wow!"

And then we had the sweetest time of fellowship, as he shared about his ministry to special-needs adults with a Christian organization down the street. The whole transaction maybe took all of ten to twelve minutes, but it was just long enough for God to jump in and do His miracle in this man's heart.

One of the most dramatic encounters we had involved a potential suicide. I got a call from a lady in upstate New York who had found our M&K Ministry website. Her daughter Tanya had just moved to Murfreesboro a month previous and was suicidal and could we do something to help? The daughter had, in her mind, set the date for her intended demise and told her mom she just had to get some things in order first before she killed herself. I called Minna to pray and discuss what we should do. I gave the mom a suicide prevention hotline number, the local counseling center contact info (though no one was there because it was a holiday) and gave her permission to give her daughter my home phone number. Four hours later, I got a phone call from Tanya asking if she could talk. After she poured out her story, I asked if I could pray with her. Very quickly, she was able to go to half-a-dozen painful memories, release the pain to the Lord, and forgive several people who had wronged her. In an hour-and-a-half she went from despair to hope, from believing God had abandoned her to praising Him for being by her side. When we were done, I asked her about the "set date," and she responded, "Jesus says it's not about death, but about life." We never heard from her or her mother again.

March 9, 2002, I put on a birthday party for Minna. Her Little Ones loved it.

CHAPTER TWENTY

Karen

> **Journal, March 9, 2002.** Minna and I have an intensive prayer time with an out-of-town AMK who's an S.R.A. victim. Uncovering horrible memories is draining. Minna, meanwhile, is dealing with her own triggers that are too horrible to mention. If she were not such a strong person, and able to hold her emotions in check, this would never work. But God's presence has been so evident and real in both their lives. I'm feeling exhaustion. Burnout. So much has been crammed into my life this past week and a half, I can't record it all. A few months ago, I thought it was all over with M. Now we see that we're not even a third of the way. Not discouraged so much as astonished. Can anyone be so fragmented? And how in the world are we ever to get to the end of this? Maybe "the end" is not a worthy goal. Just take whatever comes. . . .

By now we'd identified 66 Alters and about 400 Little Ones. The details of Minna's life came out in bits and pieces, often revolving around a theme. Sometimes we processed a whole set of Little Ones who were dealing with blood issues or being-tied-up memories or choking feelings. Each layer we chipped away uncovered deeper and darker secrets.

On March 12, 2002, I received this chilling, hand-written note from an Alter named "Renton."

Karen,

I was taught early what it was like to feel a mixture of pain and pleasure. The more intense the pain was, the more intense the pleasure became. With it came the infusion of adrenaline which made the feelings and sensations last longer.

The problem was that it requires more and more intensity to obtain a measure of satisfaction. So you go out looking for experiences that satisfy that growing need.

You understand what I mean when I say the hardness grows. The vision of the dead is not over and it moves me. I have placed a guard on the doors and no one else is permitted to speak. Amzie and Minna will feel nothing.

Renton

I read Renton's words but wasn't sure I fully understood them. So "Jackie" appeared to give me an example of some of his deeds. To put it mildly, I was horrified . . . speechless. Inside Minna's body and mind was an Alter capable of destroying me and my family, and I was on a first-name basis with him! With this new knowledge came doubt. Was I required by law to report crimes to the authorities? Was I insane to work, alone, with this person? What would Minna think when I reported Jackie's words to her. What would Scott say if he knew?

Following much prayer, Minna and I concluded we had come too far to turn back now, so we forged ahead. This was God's work, and He was orchestrating every aspect of the healing process. He was in charge of renewing Minna's mind. My job was to trust Him and be obedient.

I was reminded of 1 Corinthians 6:9-11 (NASB).

> *Or do you not know that the unrighteous will not inherit the kingdom of God? Do not be deceived; neither fornicators, nor idolaters, nor adulterers, nor effeminate, nor homosexuals, nor thieves, nor the covetous, nor drunkards, nor revilers, nor swindlers will inherit the kingdom of God. Such were some of you; but you were washed, but you were sanctified, but you were justified in the name of the Lord Jesus Christ and in the Spirit of our God.*

Every time I thought I'd heard the worst, the next story topped it. One night of intense spiritual warfare climaxed with a showdown of God's power vs. Minna's guardian personality she called The Evil One. When we finally gained access to the Little One, Jesus asked him, "Do you belong to Satan?"

The child said, "Yes."

Jesus then asked, "Do you want to belong to Me?"

The child answered, "Yes."

Jesus responded, "Then I will buy you back!"

I choked up at that one. It reminded me of an old hymn.

Redeemed, how I love to proclaim it.
Redeemed by the blood of the Lamb!
Redeemed through His infinite mercy
His child and forever I am.

By September, I felt more at peace as my own triggers occurred less frequently. God's presence was so real, so "there" all the time. I felt more rooted in my inner spirit, and my love for Jesus deepened beyond anything I could ever hope for or dream of.

Someone once said, "There are two important days in each person's life: the day you are born and the day you discover why you were born." That second day for me was really a process, a gradual realization that I had finally found my niche—I had figured out what I wanted to be when I grew up. Adulthood is only achieved as far as childhood wounds are healed.

Half a year later, I started a new phase in my healing journey. I discovered the power of processing troubling dreams. Every morning when I woke up, I tried to identify what I was feeling in my dream, followed the emotion back to a memory, and asked Jesus to come in and speak truth to that memory. It blew me away at how this worked. Such a simple tool, yet so powerful.

One morning I remember waking up with a familiar recurring dream—a borderline nightmare. Heart-pounding, trying desperately to get somewhere on time, obstacles in the way, I'm late, scrambling, always rushing. This dream occurred in various settings, but the emotion was always the same. I recalled the day almost 25 years ago when I overslept and almost missed the trip to a teachers' convention—a real panic, an adrenaline rush. As I embraced the feeling, it felt like a huge bowl tipped over and spilled its contents, and the panic drained away. I never dreamt it again.

Meanwhile, the more healing Minna received, the more drastically she changed. Her eyes became less intense. Her personality softened, and the rage began to dissipate.

My husband was pleased with the changes he saw in Minna, but when he noticed that I was changing as well, it made him feel very uncomfortable. I became more assertive, and he could no longer push so many of my buttons. He didn't know how to respond. To his credit, he began to change as well — for the better. The Lord gave me a visual of that phenomenon. It's like two people who are sitting on opposite ends of a teeter-totter. When one person moves toward the center, the other person has to move in order to adjust the balance. If God is at the center or fulcrum of the seesaw, then the closer we move toward Him, the better our relationship becomes with each other. (Of course the spouse might choose to get off the plank and leave, but that's still his choice.) If one is sitting in the center of the fulcrum, it doesn't matter what the other person does — it won't upset one's balance.

My college daughter also noticed the change in me. She has always been sensitive to my feelings, and she could hear the weight of my experiences in the tone of my voice. While she recognized that change was a good thing (she said I became more patient and a better listener), there was something very disconcerting about her mom turning into a different person. She could no longer predict how I would react in certain situations or to things she said.

For three years now, Minna and I had met together several times a week, sometimes for hours at a time, filling notebook after notebook, accessing over a thousand different parts. I listened to story after story of evil that was beyond my imagination to comprehend, but somehow God gave me the strength to stay the course.

One challenge we sometimes faced was how to deal with memories that had been lost on the left side of her brain due to her car accident. She still carried some of the emotions from them, but we had no way of accessing the memories. And so we learned how to pray and ask God to cover those and release her from the pain and give her truth.

I watched Minna's amazing, determined resolve to complete what she had started. Little by little, she chipped away the inner system of Alters and Little Ones until . . . one day we uncovered "Little Minna." Until that moment, I had not understood what "The Core Child" meant. This inner child is the one from whom all the other Little Ones originally separated. The one you're left with after everyone has integrated and there's no other personality left. Usually she hides so deep inside the Alter System that no one can find her until the others have processed their pain. "Little Minna" was the center of the diamond in her Alter System.

CHAPTER TWENTY-ONE

Karen

Journal, April 18, 2004. I sense we're on the brink of something big with Minna. And I don't know how to prepare for it—physically or emotionally. I don't understand what's going on—but when did I ever think I did!? Here's what I envision: all the Little Ones and Alters integrate. I'm left with a little five-year-old, with a will of her own and decisions to make about life and she will need parenting. And who's going to step in and adopt her? She can't function on her own—working, paying bills. How does my husband fit into this?

And I question God's motives in bringing Minna this far in her journey without a purpose. My faith is strong enough, I think, to accept His reasons whether or not I understand them. As Minna says, maybe this is all for my sake—to teach me.

But what of all the people who know her? How will this affect them? How does one explain to them what's happened? What if she really does "crack"? Can God put the pieces back together again? He can if He wants to. Am I willing to go through this journey? Do I have a choice?

On this day the entire inner system of Alters as we knew it and all the Little Ones chose to merge, leaving behind the Core Child, aged five, and to my great relief, one Guardian (surprisingly, Lane—who I thought had already merged) to help her function in the real world. It was at this point that I was shocked to discover that "Big Minna" (the

Host personality I had known all along and that presented to the world) was merely an Alter or Guardian—and she herself had been kept from this knowledge until now. The Alters had expressed fear that the brain would go insane if they disappeared, and the body would be left an imbecile. But they would not stop now—they'd made up their minds. They all had great courage and took the chance. Lane described the integration process as feeling like his brain went from holding a huge barrel full of stuff to there being only a teaspoon left. The diamond we uncovered may have been small, but it was full of light.

And, surprisingly, I began to grieve. For three years I'd developed an intensely personal relationship with Big Minna. I'd listened to the most gruesome details imaginable, watched her deep suffering, and prayed with her for hundreds of hours. It felt like I had just lost my dearest friend, never to see her again. Lane saw my tears and said, "Before everyone integrated, Big Minna told me to tell you, 'The arms of our heart will always be around you.'" Somehow I felt comforted.

Minna and I have always known that God's timing is impeccable. But it didn't feel like that at first. We were scheduled to make a trip together to Holland, Michigan, that week to facilitate some inner healing prayer training. Minna is the long-distance driver, not me, and how was I to drive ten hours with an "adult-child" beside me?

"Not to worry," Lane assured me. He'd do the driving.

But the most astonishing thing happened as we made our way up North. Little Minna asked questions—lots of them. And I began to teach. I discovered fairly quickly that she didn't know how to read, so I began with the alphabet, pointing out signs along the way. By the time we'd reached our destination, she had the reading capability of an adult. "How is that possible?" I asked Lane. He explained that all the knowledge she'd ever acquired over her lifetime was already in the brain. All she had to do was learn how to make the connections to those parts of the mind. It was merely the process she had to go through as the parts merged.

Over the next few weeks, as Little Minna grew to full maturity, Lane slowly faded away, no longer needed for his services. And to my great delight, I realized one day that "Minna" as I'd known her was fully back—only this Minna was different somehow. Softer, richer, and fuller in a three-dimensional sort of way.

Minna

Growing up inside was overwhelming—like a whole bunch of light bulbs flashing on at once. Like being bombarded with too much data. Everything was new and fresh and bright. Having to figure life out all over again because the people inside who knew the information were gone. Having to learn new pathways in the mind to connect things. Trying to figure out how to write when I had so much to write and so much to say. Jumbled thoughts. Words that came tumbling out. Sometimes I felt frustrated because I couldn't do things as quickly as I wanted to. It took a long time before everything sorted itself out. It felt like ages.

Karen

Minna's health began to decline after the integration (she started using a walking cane); and when she could no longer maintain a job, she applied for SSI. She has struggled with fibromyalgia all her life (a common response to physical trauma in abuse victims). Part of the application process included an interview with a psychiatrist. It had been fifteen months of experiencing a mono-mind, so we figured she couldn't count on qualifying for mental health disability. The psychiatrist would not permit me to be present while he examined Minna, so he surprised me when he came to the waiting room and declared, "Your friend is 'doing something.' Could you come in please?" I found Minna curled up in a fetal position on a couch. Immediately I recognized that a Little One was out. I asked the examiner's permission to pray with her (I'm sure I astonished him at the request); and within a few minutes we'd gone to a memory, the Lord spoke truth, and "Minna" returned. I laughed at God's timing. If ever the psychiatrist needed proof that Minna needed help, this would have done it.

Minna felt very disappointed when I told her what happened. But that incident made us realize once again that we could never place our stake in the ground and declare complete healing. It was another beginning, but not a starting over. The work we'd done in the past was complete, but we needed to continue to yield our hearts to God's loving care.

Minna

Life, for me, was still a crazy roller coaster ride. As time went on, however, the highs became higher and the deeps weren't as deep. On the downside, the more healing I got, the harder it was to go to memories. I needed to address the ones in which I had not dissociated. I had to force myself because I felt tired. Sheer will power and strong determination made me move forward, or I would have been stuck. I wrote the following.

What do I feel?

I don't know what I am feeling or even how to begin. I am not sure I know how to express the pain I feel inside. All I know is that it is too much to bear anymore. How do you describe emotion so deep it feels like it is killing you slowly? The pain in my throat and chest is suffocating.

Loss beyond comprehension
Despair that leaves my world black
Hurt that sears the very core of my soul
Grief that chokes the whole body
Pain . . . such deep convulsive pain.

Oh God! If only I could be released from this torment.
I search for peace and joy but it eludes me.
No matter where I turn, I cannot find it.
I feel my very soul bow down to pain's demands.
It has no mercy as it drags me beneath the earth.
The voice of God has turned away from me.
I seek His face, but He turns from me
and will not grant me peace.
I call to Him in my torment,
but He will not hear me. He is far from me!

On August 8, 2004, I began listening to some of my choir tapes from Prairie High School. Shortly after I'd sung in that elite choir, overnight—just like that—I lost my singing voice. In fact, because people in church kept asking why I wouldn't sing, I quit going to church. I believed that God had taken my talent away because I'd been bad and didn't deserve it. I felt empty. God had taken away my talent, my job, and my health. Even my mind was gone. With the damage to my brain from the car accident, I could no longer retain information like I used to. All my life I'd felt like I lived in the bottom of a well. I began to weep with deep, racking sobs of grief over a lifetime of losses and pain. This was no lie-based pain. Sorrow and grief need to be released from the cells of the body. Tears are God's creation for releasing harmful toxins. At that point, God said to me, "You know how to swim, don't you?" That brought a smile. And then He said, "You're in training." *For what?* I wondered. *What else will He take away from me?*

After that season of grief, I struggled with a very long, dry period. Karen tried to pray with me, but nothing worked like it did before. I could no longer hear from the Lord, and I began to wonder if all this healing and integration had really been worth it. In the past if I felt an emotion, I could just hand it off to an Alter or Little One to deal with it. I could still minister to other people, but if I couldn't experience any more healing myself, then I felt like a hypocrite.

In 2006 I experienced a major breakthrough. We came across a little book titled *The Shining Man with Hurt Hands* by Ellis Skolfield. The author ministered in chat rooms to people with D.I.D. using something he called "The Inner Landscape"—a visual place where the alternate personalities lived and spiritual battles were fought. Some people perceived their inner world as having rooms, caves, or tree houses. One Japanese lady lived in pagodas. Each landscape contained some form of moving water. It was very different from what we'd learned in inner healing prayer, but we decided to experiment with it. It made sense to me because I understood the concept—I felt like I'd been there before. I showed Karen a story about my quest for healing and freedom that I'd written back in 1995 (see Appendix). It took place in my inner landscape—a place as real to me as my outer world.

Once more, God had given us the tool we needed at just the right time to continue my healing journey. Now that I knew how to get to this point in my inner landscape, I revisited it several times. I discovered a waterfall and a lake made of Living Water. I tasted the smooth, silky liquid and I swam in it. And I experienced a miracle. The pain in my back suddenly disappeared. I haven't used a cane since.

CHAPTER TWENTY-TWO

Karen

I have to admit that part of me felt jealous of Minna's depth of spiritual insight, but I was very thankful that I had escaped the abuse that brought her to this point. I knew I would never be able to identify with her pain and often wondered why I was so blessed with a happy childhood. It didn't seem fair to either of us. But I've learned to trust that our loving heavenly Father has chosen each of us for a purpose — to bring glory to His name.

I remember in high school before I went on a date, a friend instructed me to "just be yourself." I had no clue at the time what that meant, but I think I've finally figured it out.

Over time I have learned how to distance myself from people's pain and to let them take responsibility for their own "stuff." I've finally broken the need-to fix-people bond that counselors term *codependency*.

Minna says I'm a softer, gentler person now. That chin-up, head-erect, stiff-back presentation is relaxed at last. My daughters say they grew up with a matter-of-fact, straight-forward, just-get-over-it mom. Now they say I speak so casually of emotional healing — like it's normal. I've shed a lot of internal anger, fear, grief, and most of all pride. My relationship with God is more personal and intimate. I still don't have the gift of observation, but with practice I've become more aware and in tune with people's pain. My conversation grid has permanently changed to listening for emotion words.

Sometimes I wonder why God chose me for this ministry — someone with few marketable skills or worldly talents, an introverted, task-oriented, stay-at-home mom. I laugh out loud at God's sense of humor. I think He gets a lot more glory for Himself this way. If He can use me, then He can use anyone.

When I look back on our story, I just shake my head in wonder. Only God could have figured out how to bring such polar opposites together. The only common denominator between Minna and me is that we grew up on the same continent. Minna, though now a mono-mind, still thinks three-dimensionally; I'm still one-track-minded, and still think linearly.

I've also questioned why He took so long to give me the tool I needed to process my own emotions. What if I'd known about inner healing prayer when I was a young person? What difference might it have made in my life choices or the wounds I inflicted on my children because of my own issues? How many other lives could I have impacted in a more positive way? I simply take comfort in the fact that all human beings are wounded in some fashion and all in need of healing and wholeness. God's timing is always impeccable and inexplicably intertwined with our human choices.

All God looks for is a willing heart, obedient to His voice, and miracles begin to happen. I've learned that I have no wisdom in and of myself (actually, I already knew that), but I now know that if I just open my mouth, He will fill it with His wisdom. I've learned that first God calls and then He equips, and He also knows how to prepare us for the call.

I note how many times I use the word *peace* in our story. And that is good. It sums up my life verse: *Thou wilt keep* [her] *in perfect peace whose mind is stayed on Thee because* [she] *trusteth in Thee (Isaiah 26:3 KJV).*

We wonder when the next beginning will start and what the next piece of the puzzle will reveal. All we know is that we're a work in progress — diamonds in the hands of a loving Father.

Minna

One day Karen suggested we write our story down — in a book — for others to read. I thought back to that first email dialogue with her.

"What will people think of me?" But I've decided it isn't about me anymore. It's about telling God's story.

As I read back over those subsequent email dialogues with Karen, it astounds me to see what I used to be like and what the different personalities did and said. I had an inkling that I was an in-your-face kind of person, but it is extremely evident from these conversations. I cringe when I read them, because I see now how I came across to people. It helps me understand why I lost some friendships. They couldn't cope with me. I was an enigma.

I am so thankful that I had godly parents who taught me the Word of God. I regret that it took me so long to return to the God I know now. He pursued me, He loved me, He never abandoned or gave up on me. I am grateful that He led me to Karen, an unlikely pairing of opposite temperaments and childhood experiences. I'm glad that we're friends.

Karen says I've changed drastically since we first met, and she's right. Pain kept me very ego-centric, but now I see how much more outward-focused I've become. I have much greater compassion for other people's pain, but still find myself impatient when they refuse to get help when they know they need it. I have to remind myself that some people are like unripe persimmons—it's best not to pick the fruit too early. Many people have to reach critical mass before they're ready to face their issues; but once they're ready, powerful healing can take place. I cried out to God to save me when I was drowning, but I couldn't hear Him under the water. Total brokenness propelled me above the float line.

I, too, have discovered who I am inside. I was born with a teacher's heart, and my passion is to point the way to the foot of the cross. I am Minna Joy Kayser, Beloved Joy of the King of Kings. I am no longer trapped by my past. I serve a gentle, kind, and loving Master Who is angry on my behalf for the pain others inflicted upon me. I see God the Father with a twinkle in His eyes (rather like my dad's), and I never want to disappoint Him.

I still have trouble writing things down, but that's more of a brain function issue than a trigger now. I think best while talking out loud, so my part of this narrative is a result of Karen's attempts to capture my thoughts and words on paper. During my dark years, I recorded several notebooks full of poetry, some of which survived my many moves. Now that I'm free of the intense pain, I no longer seem to need that outlet.

Today I am still processing memories, but at least they're normal, everyday issues I'm dealing with. As I spend time with God, He continues to open my heart to hear truth. A part of me misses the excitement and drama of opening up the doors to the various secret places, but I'm so thankful that the emotional pain of those traumatic memories is gone forever. There's nothing like emerging from the hidden crust of that dark place into God's light. His peace overshadows everything. I now see my inner diamond as solidified and whole. Like a prism, it can refract the light of Christ; and even though God isn't finished with me yet, hopefully others can see the fruits of the Spirit shining out of me.

Was it worth the pain of turning around and facing my past experiences? Of opening those closed doors? Yes! Instead of just rehashing and reliving them, I found answers, I found truth, and now I'm free at last . . . except that I'm not. I bear in my body the scars of my abuse. My health is broken. Because of my disabilities I'm dependent on others to care for my financial needs. My mind and memory, once photographic, is rapidly deteriorating. I'm becoming a prisoner once again. Flashes of anger, fragments of the past, continue to plague me, and sometimes I feel like withdrawing forever from society. The log cabin in the woods still beckons me. But I refuse to give up. I am learning how to depend on God for my every need. I am determined to allow Him to use my story to help others.

EPILOGUE

Minna and Karen

We lost count, but we know that in the first ten years we put in over a thousand hours with over 200 people. They were not all AMKs. Many were people in the community who heard of us by word of mouth, and some contacted us from out of state through our website. Some MKs and missionaries have come to stay with us for a week or more at a time for intensive prayer sessions. We pray by phone, by Skype, and in person, depending on the need and the stability of the person. One AMK is now living with Minna, going through her own healing journey from S.R.A. Others have been brought into our lives for a brief time and then moved on. We've worked with people who have experienced a variety of issues, including grief and loss, depression, phobias, addictions, abuse of all kinds, many who are D.I.D., and eight or nine who are S.R.A. victims. Each one is a miracle story of God's healing grace. Meanwhile, we continue to pursue our own mind renewal, for we know that this process will not be complete until we see Jesus face to face.

APPENDIX

Many who are dissociated have an inner landscape—a visual world of reality where the alternate personalities live. It often contains a safe place in the mind, such as a field of flowers or a waterfall. Some contain various rooms or a cave where Little Ones are housed until they're freed. Minna wrote this piece in 1995.

My Inner World

I am on a grassy hill. There is a tree behind me, but I cannot really see it. In front of me is a doorway framed in stone, like a castle entrance laid into the hillside. I enter the door and see stone stairs leading down. I go down and the stairway curves to the right. It is dimly lit by an unknown source. At the bottom, I enter a room. The floor, walls, and ceiling are made of stone. I can't really see the floor, but I can feel that it is stone. On the floor is a foggy mist that is about two feet thick. The room is approximately 20 by 20 feet with a 30-foot ceiling. In the center of the room, floating about five feet above the floor, is a large, grey, fleshy mass shaped like a football. It is about eight feet long. I don't know how it is suspended. There does not seem to be anything holding it in place. When I touch it, it feels clammy and cold. It seems to be alive. It moves as if it is breathing, but I see no place for it to take in air.

As I run my hand along its flank, I sense emotion coming from it, taking hold of me. It seems to be trying to communicate with me. I either do not understand or do not want to. I am afraid of the emotions. They are so strong. It seems to be a prisoner with no way of escape. It is in terrible pain.

I run out of the room and back up the stairs. Once out on the grassy hill, I take stock. What is it that frightens me? I am afraid of feeling the pain. I am afraid of remembering. I think of that thing down there and wonder how it got there.

For many years now, I have not been able to do more than go to that room, repeat that experience, and wonder what is wrong with me. After each time, I come to this tree and sit under it by the stream thinking about it and chastising myself for being afraid. Nothing ever changes in that room. But, I prefer sitting by this stream in the shade of the tree feeling the warmth of the sun, hearing the bees droning, simply relaxing and trying to forget. But each day, I repeatedly enter that dungeon room and examine that ugly, clammy mass. And each time, I run from it to sit under the tree and try to forget. Well, today is going to be different. Today, I am going down there and finding out what else is there. I am going to find out what is holding the mass there and find a way to free it.

I get up again and walk to the stairway entrance. I am nervous. You know, the kind of nervous you get when you are about to go into a very dangerous place or see the principal. I stand there for a moment, and then go down to the room. Nothing has changed that I can tell. The mass has taken up all my attention in the past. Maybe I should see if there is something in the room that I did not notice before.

I am a very methodical person, so I start at the stairs and begin to walk slowly around the perimeter of the room, examining the walls. I have examined three walls and have started on the fourth when I see an arched exit. I peer through but can see nothing but darkness. It seems to be stairs rather than a hallway. But it is hard to tell because it is dark. I see the mist flowing out through that exit and disappearing as it flows down. OK. Take note. There is a second access point to the room. That is a little unnerving. Someone could have been watching me through there and I would not have known it.

I hurry past the opening, feeling like some creature might reach out and grab me as I go by. I finish examining the fourth wall and proceed to cross the room in grid format to see if I can find anything on the floor. I have decided to examine under the mass last, since I don't really like being near it. I find nothing. I scan the ceiling for anything I may have missed. Nothing! So, that means I should probably go through that other doorway and find out where it leads.

After pondering that idea for a while, I decide that I really need to go up and see grass and trees and feel the sun and breeze again. I am just too uncomfortable going wherever that doorway leads. Maybe I will feel like exploring it after being refreshed by clean air. The air down here is pretty damp and musty.

So, I go back up to my tree and sit to ponder the situation and reflect on what I have found. I am sure there was only one door into the room before. I shiver with a sudden chill and the certain knowledge that those creatures I sense are very real and can do interesting things to my landscape.

OK. I have to do this. I might be only six years old, but I have to do this anyway. No one else can do it for me. I go back down to the room. I glance at the mass to see if there is any change. Nothing. OK. It is now or never. Gathering up all my courage, I approach the opening and peer in. It appears to be stairs. I can't just step out into that. The steps might be broken. I could fall and hurt myself and there would be no one to rescue me.

I look around the room again to see if there is something I can poke the steps with. In the corner is a staff leaning against the wall. That wasn't there earlier. I get a crawling sensation on my skin. Someone must be here and I can't see them. I think about the mist. They could be hiding in it. If I go to the corner for the staff, they could grab my ankle. I swallow hard and set my jaw. If they do, I will fight like never before!

I go to the corner and grab the staff. Quickly I stir the mist with the staff. There is nothing within reach of the staff. That gives me a little more courage. I approach the doorway again and peer through. Sigh! I guess I am hoping there might be some light now since things seem to appear when I need them. Using the stick to probe the darkness, I make my way down the stairs. I move the stick back and forth to feel the sides of the stairwell and touch the step to make sure it is there before making each move. This is slow and tedious work and it takes a long time. Counting each step helps to keep my mind off thoughts of running into nasty creatures.

At the count of one hundred and forty-two, I discover I am at the bottom. There is a lot of mist here, and a torch is on the wall burning dimly. Looking around, I see that I am on a sort of platform or stone dock beside an underground river. There is a rowboat tied to the dock with oars in it. As I look left, I see that the tunnel, or cave, disappears into a thick blackness. I say thick because it seems to be a palpable, heavy darkness that pushes back against the light. Straight ahead, I see the stone of the opposite wall. To my right, downstream, it is dark, but seems like the kind of darkness that will back off when light is brought to it. The river seems to be flowing fairly fast and strong.

What should I do now? If I get into the boat, I don't know if I can get back. Maybe I should just go back upstairs and think this over.

I hear something to my left and quickly turn to see what it is. There is a strange creature there. It is standing awkwardly and kicking at the ground as if it is shy about being discovered. I say "it" because it is hard to tell if it is a male or female. I find my heart pounding as I ask it who it is.

"I am Chador. You should not have come here," it says.

"Why not? I am exploring, trying to find a way to help Mass," I respond.

"Mass does not need help. Mass is there because it is safe there," It replies.

"Where does the river come from, and where does it go?" I ask it.

"I cannot say where it comes from, but it goes outside where there is light," It says.

"I am too small to take the boat. Will you take me outside?" I ask.

Chador gets a small smile on its face and looks a little hopeful. "I will take you if you are looking for a quiet, safe place to stay," It responds.

I quickly get into the boat and settle myself. It takes the torch and places it on the bow of the boat, gets in, unties the boat and pushes off. It does not paddle much since the current is taking us rather fast through the tunnel. It seems to be an expert, knowing exactly when to change course even though I cannot see the need. I know that, if I were navigating, we would have hit the walls because the turns come up so fast.

Suddenly, we burst out of the tunnel into beautiful sunlight. It is breathtaking. There are green fields with wild flowers, rolling hills, and off in the distance, trees and mountains. It pulls over to the right bank and jumps out, pulling the boat up after it. There is a tree there by the river. I get out of the boat and sit down under the tree. It is so peaceful here. I feel like staying here and resting for a long time.

Karen

With Habila, my African nanny

Climbing trees was my all-time favorite activity.

Grade 6 in the USA

After I met Minna

Minna

Grade 3

*Grade 6, Sir Wm. Van Horne
Elementary School, 1968-69*

*1994, Abbotsford,
before my accident*

*June, 2001, the day Karen asked
me to email my memories to her*

Disclaimer. These are not the psychiatric or scientific definitions. These definitions are our attempt to help the layperson track with our story.

Abreaction – Body movements which reflect what is happening in the memory.

Alter (Guardian, Helper, Protector, Part) – A personality that protects or guards a Little One—often created by the mind to keep the L.O. hidden in order to prevent more pain. The Alter can grow in age and maturity over time.

Alter System – The inner perception of how the Alters and Little Ones are ordered in the mind.

Core Child – The original child within who got stunted in mental and emotional growth due to trauma. The one from whom all the Little Ones originally separated. The one you're left with after everyone has integrated and there's no other Alternate Personality left. Often has the same name as the host.

D.I.D. (Dissociative Identity Disorder) - Formerly termed M.P.D. (Multiple Personality Disorder) or commonly called "split personality." A psychiatric condition in which an individual switches between at least two personalities or identities. Dissociation happens DURING an event.

Dissociation – The separation of the conscious mind from the subconscious mind. The degree of dissociation occurs on a continuum from "zoning out" to full-blown D.I.D. The coping mechanism of choice for early childhood trauma.

Double Bind - A psychological predicament when contradictory demands are made of an individual so that no matter which choice is made, undesirable consequences will result.

Host - The primary person or Alter that presents to the general public. The host may or may not be co-conscious (aware) of the Alter System inside.

Inner Landscape – The inner world of reality. Often contains a safe place in the mind, such as a field of flowers or a waterfall. Sometimes contains various rooms or a cave where Little Ones are housed until they're freed.

Integration – The perceived merging of the Alters and Little Ones into the Core personality. The personalities do not "die" or disappear; they are simply given a new job within the mind.

Little One – The child part that experienced the trauma and remains stuck in the memory and time until truth is received and healing occurs. The L.O. always remains the same age.

Mind Games – psychological manipulation to control or intimidate.

Parts (Alters, Little Ones) – Various personalities or parts of the mind that have split from the core person.

Programming – Deliberate attempt by a perpetrator to split the mind for the purpose of mind control.

Split – The intentional separation of the conscious mind from the subconscious mind. It occurs when a personality is separated into two or more entities.

S.R.A. (Satanic Ritual Abuse) – Intentional and systematic abuse by evil perpetrators, often for the purpose of mind control. Involves elements of child sacrifice, sexual abuse, double-binds, demonization, and desecration of the sacraments.

Switching - The process of changing from one Alter/personality to another. The process varies from one system to another. Some people get headaches if they switch too quickly.

Resources

If you would like to talk to someone right now about a personal relationship with Jesus Christ, please call toll-free 1-888-NEED HIM (1-888-633-3446).

Disclaimer: M&K Ministry does not necessarily endorse the content on all of these sites.

Blessing or Curse — You Can Choose, By Derek Prince
This book helped us understand the power of our words and actions and how they can bind us.
Derekprince.org

Freedom in Christ Ministries (FICM), founded by Dr. Neil T. Anderson
Dr. Anderson is the bestselling author or coauthor of more than 60 books, including *The Bondage Breaker: Overcoming Negative Thoughts, Irrational Feelings, Habitual Sins*
ficm.org

It's Only a Demon, by David Appleby
Gives a detailed discussion on the subject of demons and deliverance. Answers the question, "What do I do now that I've tried everything else and nothing works?"
spiritualinterventions.org

M&K Ministry
That's us!
mkministry.org

Restoration in Christ Ministries, founded by Dr. Tom R. Hawkins
This organization ministers to S.R.A. victims. Their material was quite helpful to us. "RCM offers training and support to those called to restore lives shattered by abuse." Dr. Hawkin's wife has carried on the ministry since her husband's death.
rcm-usa.org

Restoring the Heart Ministries, founded by Julie Woodley
"Our primary purpose is to help men, women, and children find freedom and hope from the life experience of emotional, sexual and physical abuse, as well as other types of trauma."
rthm.cc

144

Sozo
A unique inner healing and deliverance ministry aimed to get to the root of things hindering your personal connection with the Father, Son and Holy Spirit.
bethelsozo.com

Spiritual Warfare, by Dr. Karl Payne
Karl Payne is the pastor of Leadership Development and Discipleship at Antioch Bible Church and Chaplain for the NFL's Seattle Seahawks. "He has written a guidebook for defense that is simple, biblical, and transferable. Through his teaching on how to recognize and resolve attacks from the world, we learn that we are more than conquerors in Christ."

Theophostic Prayer Ministry, founded by Dr. Ed Smith
Our original and primary training tool. "TPM is intentional and focused prayer with the desired outcome of an authentic encounter with the presence of Christ, resulting in mind renewal and subsequent transformed life." A free download of the first three chapters of *Healing Life's Hurts* (an introduction to TPM) is available on their website. However, please do not attempt to practice TPM on others without extensive training.
theophostic.com

The Shining Man with Hurt Hands, by Ellis Skolfield
Anecdotal experiences of working online with D.I.D. clients using their Inner Landscape. A copy of the book is available in pdf format.
fishhouseministries.com/index.htm

Third Culture Kids: Growing Up Among Worlds, by Dave C. Polluck and Ruth E. Van Reken
Dave (now deceased) and Ruth are cutting-edge researchers on all things cross-cultural. Ruth speaks nationally and internationally on issues related to global family living and is co-founder of Families in Global Transition. She also authored **Letters Never Sent.**
crossculturalkid.org/

Too Small to Ignore, by Wes Stafford, former president of Compassion International. An MK story of triumph over abuse.
toosmalltoignore.com

29930117R00090

Made in the USA
San Bernardino, CA
01 February 2016